IN PURSUIT OF HEALTHY-NESS

How I Reinvented My Life with Intermittent Fasting

Connie Ragen Green

In Pursuit of Healthy-ness:
How I Reinvented My Life with Intermittent Fasting
Connie Ragen Green

Copyright © 2021 by Hunter's Moon Publishing
ISBN Paperback: 978-1-937988-57-9
ISBN eBook: 978-1-937988-58-6

Hunter's Moon Publishing
https://HuntersMoonPublishing.com
Hunter's Moon Publishing - Connie Ragen Green
P.O. Box 3295
Santa Barbara, CA 93130-3295

Connie Ragen Green - ConnieRagenGreen.com

CONNIE RAGEN GREEN'S TITLES

- ☼ Book Launch Booster Rockets: *Helping Your Prospects to Find You Everywhere*
- ☼ Speakers! The Quick Public Speaking to Business Method™ - *Turning Your Talk into an Ongoing Revenue Stream*
- ☼ The Road Trip: *An Entrepreneur's Journey of Self-Discovery*
- ☼ Authors! The Quick Book to Business Method™ - *Turning Your Book into an Ongoing Revenue Stream*
- ☼ Local Business Marketing: *Making the Phone Ring for Businesses Everywhere*
- ☼ Doing What It Takes: *The Online Entrepreneur's Playbook*
- ☼ Kids and Money – *Teaching Financial Responsibility and Values to Children*
- ☼ Rethinking the Work Ethic: *Embrace the Struggle and Exceed Your Own Potential*
- ☼ The Transformational Entrepreneur: *Creating a Life of Dedication and Service*
- ☼ *Book. Blog. Broadcast. The Trifecta of Entrepreneurial Success*
- ☼ Write. Publish. Prosper. *How to Write Prolifically, Publish Globally, and Prosper Eternally*
- ☼ Living the Internet Lifestyle: *Quit Your Job, Become an Entrepreneur, and Live Your Ideal Life*
- ☼ The Inner Game of Internet Marketing – *with Geoff Hoff*
- ☼ The Weekend Marketer: *Say Goodbye to the '9 to 5', Build an Online Business, and Live the Life You Love*
- ☼ Time Management Strategies for Entrepreneurs: *How to Manage Your Time to Increase Your Bottom Line* – *with Geoff Hoff*
- ☼ Huge Profits with Affiliate Marketing: *How to Build an Online Empire by Recommending What You Love*
- ☼ Huge Profits with a Tiny List: *50 Ways to Use Relationship Marketing to Increase Your Bottom Line*

… and too many more to mention!

DEDICATION

This book is dedicated to the five people who have been most instrumental in my success with my journey back to optimal health with intermittent fasting, in assisting me with a shift in my mindset, and in helping me to learn how to once again move my body and feel comfortable in my skin.

Denise Wakeman is one of the first people I met when I came online to start a business in 2006. At that time, she was already an entrepreneur and thought leader in her own right. She had begun running and as a former runner I followed her journey in this area. I connected with her professionally when she offered a three-month training on building, growing, and developing an online presence through blogging.

I came aboard for Denise's training, believing that I already knew everything there was to know on this topic. On the first day I realized I was operating in the state of "Unconscious Incompetence" and still had much to learn. I buckled in for the ride and was able to begin building my business based on the strategies, methods, and values she instilled in me. She talked about our target audience being able to find us everywhere and it wasn't long before this became my reality. To this day, I blog regularly on three separate sites.

Dr. Ellen Britt, PA, Ed.D. is someone I have known since my second year online. She was helping newer entrepreneurs like myself make a name for ourselves with telesummits, social media, and more and I was anxious to learn from her.

At some point I learned that she had worked for years as a Physician Assistant and that all things related to health was her primary interest.

Denise and Dr. Ellen teamed up to teach about intermittent fasting several years ago. They are both living this lifestyle each day and sharing every detail of what is working for them. I joined their more general group on Facebook but did not think seriously about intermittent fasting until March of 2020.

Dr. Bassem El Tom became my physician in January of 2020. It didn't take long for me to realize that he was a diamond in the rough and that I would now be able to access the best medical care available in the United States through him and his team. He goes above and beyond when it comes to my health, and I know he is doing this not only for me, but for all of his patients.

When we met in person for the first time in March of 2020, I shared with him that I was beginning to learn about and ready to start a practice of intermittent fasting. He was knowledgeable about this and encouraged me to move forward. He recommended that I have blood work done every three months to track how my body was adjusting. Throughout this journey, he has continued to be supportive and advises me from his perspective as my physician.

Cheryl A. Major, CNWC is someone I greatly admire and consider as my primary source for nutritional information. She is the person who made me become more mindful of what I was eating so I could replace the habits that were not serving me with ones that helped me to become strong and healthy. She leads by example every single day.

It was the release of her first book, *Eat Your Blues Away: "Disappearing" Depression by Changing What You Eat* that made me realize how powerful her message is to everyone who has struggled with health issues and maintaining a healthy weight, as well as the power of what we eat in regards to our mental health.

I met Kathy Hicks online in April of 2020 and became a part of her daily workout program. She continues to help me develop a strong, flexible, and resilient body and mind.

Kathy has a way of observing the behavior and body movements of those she works with, and then honing in on the parts of the body we each need more help with improving. Her feet fitness training and exercises have given me a much-needed reset when it comes to walking and hiking. I'm now light on my feet and amazed that I once thought these activities could only be a part of my past.

These five people have become the fabric of my life over the past couple of years. They have each been a piece of my health and wellness puzzle and I owe them my life.

This work is also dedicated to everyone who has struggled with being overweight, attempted serious weight loss, and experienced related health issues at any point in your lifetime. I know firsthand what this is like. I also know that turning your life around is possible.

May you be healthy, strong, and confident and may your journey be one that opens up an entire new way of eating, moving, living, and simply *being* that serves you in a joyous and optimal way.

FOREWORDS

Connie Green's IF Journey: 5 Principles She Used to Succeed

When Connie Green makes a decision to do something, she goes all in. When I met Connie in 2006, she had just begun her journey of building an online business. She'd made the decision to leave a long-time teaching career to become an entrepreneur, and so typical of Connie, she jumped in with both feet.

Since then, I've watched her build, grow, and achieve phenomenal success over the past 15 years.

One of the remarkable things about Connie is that when she takes off and runs with an idea, she takes her community with her. But more on that in a second.

Fast forward to March 2020, which looking back, was an inauspicious month in the history of the world. I was speaking at an in-person marketing event Connie was hosting.

During the course of the event, I happened to mention that my business partner, Ellen Britt, PA, Ed.D. and I were hosting our first 10-day intermittent fasting challenge.

Connie acknowledged what I said but of course moved on. After all, she was the host of this particular event and that was her focus. Later, she did ask me for details and ended up joining the challenge.

That weekend, which was the onset of the COVID-19 pandemic, turned out to be the beginning of widespread lockdowns. This was an interesting confluence of events because our first 10-day challenge coincided with this horrific pandemic that every person in the world was learning to navigate.

Many of our challenge participants were grateful for the opportunity to learn something that would benefit them during this tumultuous time.

Our Intermittent Fasting Challenge was not limited to teaching participants how to lose weight by practicing fasting. We were also introducing our students to how they could live healthier lives and improve their overall well-being.

For many people, these lessons could not have come at a better time!

True to her nature, right away Connie started applying her entrepreneurial success strategies to what she was learning about integrating a fasting practice into her life. But things weren't as easy for her as you might think.

Here's a profile of Connie before she started her journey with intermittent fasting, as she is very transparent about sharing the details of her story...

Connie weighed 302 pounds, which is in the medically morbidly obese category, and was also pre-diabetic when she joined the first 10-Day IF Challenge. She was under duress, as her doctor was threatening to start her on insulin treatment if her numbers didn't improve.

Due to her weight, Connie had lots of aches and pains and it was difficult for her to walk with ease to exercise. On top of all that, she's also a four-time cancer survivor. So, it's a huge understatement to say she was facing tremendous challenges before starting her fasting practice.

Like many other people, over the years Connie had tried all kinds of ways to lose weight and to improve her health, but nothing seemed to work to help her to get that weight off and keep it off. She was about ready to just give up and accept that things would never change and that her health would continue to deteriorate over time.

But then Connie was introduced to intermittent fasting, and it was like she had been handed the key to a Ferrari... she slid into the driver's seat, turned the key in the ignition, and took off!

When I say Connie goes all in, I'm not exaggerating, and her results are evident to everyone who knows her.

How did Connie do it?

The IF Challenge laid the groundwork for Connie's success because she followed these five principles:

One - She showed up consistently.

Beginning with the first day of the Challenge, Connie attended every live Q&A call, asked questions, and participated fully, implementing each of the 10 days of action prompts.

Two - She did the work.

It may not have always been comfortable for her, but Connie followed the checklist, took measurements, tracked her progress in a journal, and brought her questions both to the private Facebook group as well as the live Q&A calls. She posted and shared her experiences with her cohort, helping others as well as herself.

Three - She studied the research.

When Ellen and I shared books and research articles about the benefits of intermittent fasting, Connie read and studied them. She wasn't shy about asking for clarity on some of the science, like how autophagy works. She didn't give up until she was sure she understood.

Four - She experimented and applied the tips and suggestions.

Every day during the challenge we answered questions and gave tips and suggestions for how to manage a fasting schedule. Connie took everything to heart and experimented daily to discover how her body and mind behaved and adapted to this new way of being. She made her fasting practice her own.

Five - She figured out what worked for her unique situation.

As a pre-diabetic, Connie's situation was different from most of the other participants. She consulted with her doctors so she knew the best ways to safely and effectively apply fasting practices to her life.

As a result, just like her success in business as an internet marketer and teacher, Connie has improved with nearly every health challenge she faces and has absolutely transformed her life. I witnessed this transformation with her business over the years, and now, I have witnessed it with her health.

18 months after attending her first 10-Day Intermittent Challenge, Connie, at the moment I am writing, has lost 125 pounds through the consistent practice of intermittent fasting!

To date, she has attended every single IF challenge we have hosted (3-4 per year). She's been an active participant in our private community, the Fast Factor Circle, and she graduated from our six-month, Intermittent Fasting Coaching Certification Program so she can take her success and help others achieve the same results.

If that isn't dedication and commitment to her health, well-being and living a long, healthy life, I don't know what is. Connie is an exemplary role model for you, for me, and for her community, because she embodies the challenge of taking charge and control of her life.

Yes, Connie's story and success are remarkable. Yet, IF isn't just for people who are overweight or diabetic. And intermittent fasting isn't just for people who may have health-related challenges.

I have been practicing intermittent fasting for three years (so far), thanks to Ellen Britt's invitation after she told me her success story. When I started, I admit, like so many other people, I was in it for the weight loss.

I had about 30 pounds to lose and successfully lost that weight in the course of about eight months.

But besides weight loss, there are many more benefits to practicing intermittent fasting. For many people like Connie, Ellen, me, and hundreds of others we've worked with, it truly becomes a way of life.

For some, it sparks a change towards making healthier food choices.

For others, it moves them to explore more practices they can stack with IF to make it even more effective.

And for others who've had similar mindset shifts, they start to look at what other areas of their lives they previously thought they had no control over, as they suddenly realize they can achieve almost anything they set their minds to. All it takes is a decision to begin.

Ultimately, a consistent fasting practice can start you on the journey to a longer, healthier, more joy-filled life. What could be better than that? Just ask Connie!

Denise Wakeman
Founder, Marketing Trailblazers Community
CoFounder, The Fast Factor

Overcoming a Lifetime of Obesity, As Well as Reversing Type 2 Prediabetes

When Connie asked me if I would be willing to write the Foreword for her new book on her experience with intermittent fasting, I quickly responded with an unequivocal "Yes!" I've known Connie for over a dozen years now and first had the pleasure of meeting her in 2008 at an internet marketing conference in Atlanta.

I'll never forget that first meeting because Connie impressed me as someone who was not only already having considerable success with internet marketing but I also could immediately tell she was going to go on to be a powerhouse in the internet marketing space. Connie carried herself with confidence and spoke clearly and succinctly about her prior experience as a teacher and what her goals were as she moved into this new arena.

I was at that conference because I was trying to educate myself about the internet marketing world. My background, like Connie's, was not in marketing, as I had come from the world of medicine. My medical experience includes two decades of practice as a PA (Physician Assistant) in emergency as well as occupational medicine, and I once conservatively estimated that over the course of my practice I had seen enough patients to fill the Houston Astrodome not once, but twice! Along the way, I completed a Master's in Clinical Psychology as well as a doctorate (an Ed.D.) in Biology.

So when I saw Connie, in spite of admiring her confidence, her ready sense of humor, and the way she carried herself, I couldn't help but see something else.

Connie was morbidly obese. This is a clinical term that we medical professionals use to classify someone whose body weight has gone beyond the merely obese and is applied to those individuals who are overweight by more than 100 pounds.

Because of my medical training and experience seeing so many patients over the course of my career, I knew that Connie's health was at great risk because of her obesity, including being susceptible to type 2 diabetes, heart disease, sleep apnea, gallstones, esophageal reflux, osteoarthritis, and cancer.

At the time I met Connie, I did not realize that she had already been diagnosed and treated for stage three breast cancer. But like every single patient I had ever had the privilege of treating, I knew that Connie, like so many other people who struggle to keep their weight under control, had likely been fighting a life-long battle with her weight.

People who are obese, unlike the way many people who are of a healthy weight tend to stereotype them, are acutely and painfully aware of their own body weight. Most of them have battled their weight for years, with moments of elation at temporary success only to see their hopes for a "normal" body come crashing down when the latest diet program fails them once again.

As a medical professional, I saw this all the time in my practice, and like so many others in the medical field, there seemed to be little to offer these patients that would prove to have lasting effects. Sure, we clinicians talked to patients about caloric restriction, the importance of exercise, and eating healthy foods. We enlisted the help of nutritionists and dieticians and in some cases as a last resort, sent these patients off to a bariatric surgeon to have an intestinal bypass or stomach band put in place.

I'll never forget the evening an obese young woman came into the emergency department in the throes of a full-blown panic attack. The reason? She was deathly afraid she was going to choke to death because she had recently undergone a medically sanctioned procedure to have her jaws wired shut in a desperate attempt to get her weight under control! So when I met Connie, I knew the road ahead for her was likely to be very rough indeed.

At that time, I knew nothing of intermittent fasting. Never in my entire life did I ever have any personal concerns about my weight, but when I hit menopause, it seemed like I could just look at a picture of food and gain ten pounds! Over the course of a few years, I packed on an extra 40 pounds, and while this weight gain was minuscule in terms of what Connie was facing, I felt miserable. And yes, I tried everything I knew to get those pounds off.

I would manage to lose a few pounds and then "the diet" would become unsustainable, I would revert to my old patterns and the pounds would come rushing back, along with a few of its friends!

At some point, I just gave up and resigned myself that this was just going to be the way it was. But one day, I stumbled into the world of intermittent fasting. Initially, like so many people, I was resistant, but once I did my research, I was convinced it was safe and that it might be the key.

So, I jumped in headfirst. Nine months of daily intermittent fasting later, I had lost 35 pounds and weighed the same thing the day I did when I graduated from college. But more important than what I lost was what I gained. My confidence in myself, which had been badly damaged, returned. My focus, my productivity, and my energy soared.

To date, I have been practicing intermittent fasting for over three years and have no plans to give it up!

When I saw that Connie had registered for our ten-day intermittent fasting challenge, I was elated. While I had hoped that Connie would find success with a practice that has brought me and so many others countless benefits, her results have absolutely astounded me. Not only is she no longer morbidly obese, but she has also reversed her type 2 diabetes and has reclaimed her health and her life. I could not be more proud of her.

Connie is the perfect person to write this book, as she has a story to tell about overcoming obesity that plagued her since she was a child. Her story is raw, transparent, and real, yet is filled with hope and lessons for anyone who needs inspiration, a role model, and needs to hear from someone who most people would have written off as "most likely to remain obese."

But this book is more than just Connie's story, as it is filled with real-world, practical advice and steps you can take to change your own health and life for the better. I commend you for reading this book and as a former clinician, I encourage you to take the lessons in this book and apply them to your own situation, whatever that may be, and whatever stage you are in life.

It is never, ever too late to make a positive change in your health. Intermittent fasting, when done correctly, is safe and effective. Daily intermittent fasting is not a diet, it's a way of life, as Connie can attest.

I have likely never met you, but I can assure you, by reading this book and taking the time to explore the path Connie took to reclaim her health and her life, you are in excellent hands. Enjoy the journey!

Ellen Britt, PA, Ed.D.
Atlanta, Georgia 2021

PREFACE

Intermittent fasting saved my life, at a time when the planet had shifted ever so slightly off its axis and the Coronavirus pandemic took hold. I'll go into much more detail about this later on, but for now suffice it to say that this situation woke me up with matters directly related to my health. I am alive today because I finally listened to my body, opened my mind to a new cache of information, beliefs, and attitude, and then assembled a team and a plan to reinvent my life.

My health issues and underlying conditions made me a candidate who would not do well if I contracted the Coronavirus. All of a sudden, I realized that it was up to me to improve my health so that the medical professionals on the front line could do their best to save my life if the need arose. I became an active participant in regards to my overall health, instead of waiting on the sidelines for the other shoe to drop.

I never could have imagined that I'd be writing a book about health, wellness, and fitness in general and more specifically, intermittent fasting as a method to lose weight and reinvent myself in a healthy and sustainable way. My background, experience, and history as an author comes in the areas of entrepreneurship, public speaking, marketing, authorship, and mindset.

Since 2010, I've penned over twenty titles in these areas to share my expertise with others, based specifically on my experiences since 2006. But, the opportunity cost of writing this book makes sense for those who will be motivated and inspired to follow in my footsteps. I'm passionate about sharing my experience and results with you!

Weight loss is an area almost everyone can relate to, but few understand. If you have ever found yourself overweight or dealing with a health issue of any type, then you know firsthand that having trustworthy people and information at your fingertips can be crucial.

I spent a good part of my first half-century of life arguing for my limitations. Do this long enough, and with consistent perseverance and you will become a master at self-sabotage. I wasn't pretty enough, smart enough, or interesting enough. I was less than everyone I encountered in my life's journey, at least in my mind.

When I began to blossom after graduating from UCLA with honors (that alone should have given me the confidence to stand tall in my power) I quickly sunk even deeper into the throes of despair at what my life could and should be, both personally and professionally.

I've tried every diet you can imagine. I've eaten only apples for three days at a time, attempted no carb, low carb, high fat, and high protein diets, and counted more calories than I care to remember. These all worked extremely well for me, but only in the short-term. Soon, my weight crept back to what it had been when I started, along with additional unwanted pounds. Add to that the shrinking of my confidence and self-esteem and you can see why I longed for a more permanent solution.

Also, gaining and losing and gaining again can wreak havoc with your overall health, aging you prematurely, and making it more difficult for you to recover from any illness or injury. The human body is awesome, as long as we do our part to stay strong.

I've written this book to help you avoid anything negative in your life in regards to your health, that you can make a difference with on your own. We live in a physical world where our outward appearance lands on others the moment we meet face to face. Whether we're connecting in person or virtually, there we are for all to see. Putting our best foot forward goes beyond the cliché as we are examined and scrutinized by our fellow humans.

Body mass and health are intertwined. Although I am not a doctor and have no medical training, I've spent decades getting to know how the human body works; specifically, my body. This journey has taken me through the hills and valleys of wellbeing, illness, injury, and back again to my search of optimal health for myself. It's my pursuit for what I think of and refer to as *healthy-ness* and what I'll be sharing with you within these pages.

Add to body weight our mental health and wellbeing, and you get the complete picture. I do not believe we can be overweight, or obese, or "morbidly" obese, as was the case with me and be of sound and healthy mind. One thing is simply not congruent with the other.

Intermittent fasting isn't new, but it continues to be a somewhat controversial topic filled with myths, misconceptions, and opinions at every turn. I originally believed this practice would require me to fast for days at a time. It turns out a very small percentage of intermittent fasters ever go for 24 hours or longer without eating real food.

I will tell you that I've lost a hundred pounds previously. It was during 2004, the year I turned forty-nine years old. I achieved this goal the old-fashioned way, meaning that I earned every pound I lost by starving by body and exercising in an extreme way.

Every couple of weeks I would go off this "diet" I had created for myself and return to the way of eating I was used to throughout much of my lifetime. It was a dangerous way to eat and live and losing weight during that time did more harm than good in the overall scheme of things.

My cholesterol, blood pressure, and A1C went up to dangerous levels, I began to have heart palpitations, and two doctors told me I would probably put back all the weight I was losing, and more, by dieting in this way. It wasn't that I didn't believe them, but more that I didn't care what they were advising me to do. I told myself that at least I wasn't taking any diet pills or supplements that could permanently harm my health.

It was during this period that I considered having gastric bypass surgery. My primary physician at that time gave me a referral to a gastroenterologist and I went for the initial consultation.

While I was in the waiting room, I spoke with three women who were there for follow up visits. By the time I went in to speak with the doctor, I had already decided not to go through with the surgery for a variety of reasons.

As I drove home that day, I can remember feeling very sad and alone. I honestly believed that staying on my low-calorie diet and exercising as much as possible was the best way for me to drop the hundred extra pounds I had been asking my body to support for me.

I did achieve that goal, and the weight began to creep back on beginning the following day. I felt helpless in my struggle to maintain a healthy weight and knew that this issue was my weakness in life. My goal then became to only allow myself to gain ten or twenty pounds and then starve myself until I lost some of it again.

This yo-yo dieting was reminiscent of my teenage years. I knew it was not a solution to a much deeper problem, that it was only a band-aid for something that needed to be addressed in a different way. But I felt powerless in this area of my life and allowed my weight to affect every other area in the process.

It wasn't until sixteen years later that I would discover intermittent fasting. This revelation came quite by chance, and only because I knew two people who were having great success with it and helping others to do the same. These people are ones I will mention and refer to throughout this book – Dr. Ellen Britt, PA, Ed.D. and Denise Wakeman, friends and colleagues who are helping me and thousands of others to change our lives forever, in a healthy and permanent way. These women, along with my personal physician, Dr. Bassem El Tom are the people I turn to regularly to make sure what I am doing in my IF practice is serving me in a holistic way.

Contents

INTRODUCTION

"He who has health has hope; and he who has hope, has everything."

~ Thomas Carlyle

I'd like for you to think of this book as a guide and blueprint to your improved health and renewed youthfulness. I will reiterate that I am not a doctor or a medical professional of any kind. Instead, I've been in charge of the care and feeding of my human body for six decades now. What I'm sharing with you changed my life in many ways and continues to ensure that my future is bright and my body strong and healthy.

It was as though most of the people I encountered in my earlier life knew a secret that eluded me. Over the years I made a study of people in general, and it went back to the time my 8th grade English teacher, Exum Kranick described herself as someone who "ate to live" rather than one who "lived to eat."

Mrs. Kranick was what I describe as being "pencil thin" and I believe she must have been this way her entire life. I met her just at the time when I was beginning to feel left out of social activities and much more because I was overweight.

I experimented with "eating to live" but it did not resonate with me. I was a foodie before that label came into vogue.

In the first section of this book, I define what "healthy-ness" means to me. This is a personal journey, so what's important and stands out to me may be a little, or even a lot different than what you are thinking. My goal here is not to persuade you to change your beliefs and values around this specific area of health and wellness, but instead to learn more about what is possible when you embrace and incorporate intermittent fasting into your life to one degree or another.

In the first chapter we embark on a journey through time to explore the history of intermittent fasting. I move as to the concept of "food as fuel" in the second chapter, the then jump into my story of the years I spent going up and down with my weight during the third chapter.

Why your health must be a priority is the theme of the second section. I discuss surrendering in the rawest sense in the fourth chapter, and why I believe that health and wellness naturally go together in chapter five. In chapter six I introduce you to the anti-aging benefits of intermittent fasting. This includes a discuss of something called "autophagy" that continues to be a primary goal and focus of my own IF practice.

We move on to the "What If?" stage of intermittent fasting in the third section. I discuss a new way of eating and of "being", as well as the idea of how I am paying it forward with the knowledge and experience I'm developing and expanding upon each day.

The fourth section is where I share my thoughts on how you can get started with intermittent fasting, based on my experiences, as well as how to reinvent yourself with this lifestyle. Then I discuss how to live a full life as an intermittent faster, and how to get back on track when you get derailed for any reason at all.

"What's Next for You?" is the theme of my fifth and final section and I hope you will understand how all of this can come together for you and be beneficial to you in untold ways.

PROLOGUE

I *hadn't seen Lynne and Eddie since they were children. They are siblings who used to spend their summers with my family over three decades ago. Now they were living in Snellville, Georgia with spouses and children of their own.*

When I arrived, I could smell the food cooking and hear the sounds coming from the kitchen. Lynn had promised to create some special dishes from the vegetables she was growing outside in the garden. Eddie appeared from another part of the house, taking my suitcase and guiding me into the dining room. He pulled out the chair at the head of the table and I sat down.

As soon as I was seated, I heard the sound made by a wobbly chair leg that was being asked to support too much weight. More sounds followed, each incrementally more ominous than the initial one and within a few seconds the wooden high back chair was crashing to the floor.

Eddie caught my arm on the way down, allowing me to graciously regain my balance. I was embarrassed, of course. Lynne's son, Matthew was summoned to pick up the pieces and take them out to the trash pile. A new chair appeared, this one much sturdier than the first and we all sat down to eat. No one mentioned what had happened during the remainder of my visit, but it was the elephant in the room, to be sure.

This incident occurred in 1999, yet it would be two decades before I took it as a sign that the part of my life that involved my health was out of control.

SECTION ONE

DEFINING HEALTHY-NESS

"Happiness lies, first of all, in health."

~ George William Curtis

No one gets to a body weight of over three hundred pounds overnight, or even within a decade. Amassing this kind of weight takes time, effort, commitment, and planning, along with a willingness to throw caution to the wind. And you cannot possibly grow tall enough for that weight to ever be in the normal range, especially if you're already a full grown, adult human.

The chubby baby and toddler becomes an awkward school-age child who is self-conscious and less likely to take the risks associated with success. The obese teen must deal with the psychological issues and social stigmas around body image, and then becomes a sedentary adult with health issues and a proclivity towards negative thinking. This is only a part of this situation. Overweight children, teens and adults are more likely to have low self-esteem and fewer friends, and to not do as well in school as their counterparts who are living at a healthy weight for their height and build.

I define *healthy-ness* to mean the state of feeling comfortable in your skin, and the ability to physically, mentally, and emotionally create a life that brings you joy and satisfaction.

Being able to cross my legs when I sit down, to put on shoes and socks without having to carefully lift each leg up and to the side to accomplish this, and to sit cross-legged on my bed or on the floor with my dogs and grandkids beside me are all non-scalable victories I do not take for granted. I'll talk more about these "non-scalable victories" or "NSVs" later on in this book.

Also, it turns out I was literally a "fat head" for many years. Once I dropped about fifty pounds, I became aware that my glasses and hats fit better and I appeared to conform when I saw photos of myself with others. It turns out that subcutaneous fat on your head is really a thing. Who knew?!

I have discovered that whereas the overwhelming majority of people are motivated and influenced with their eating, exercising, and other health practices by the pursuit of happiness to take certain actions, a much smaller percentage of people are influenced by the pursuit of healthiness, or as I prefer to think of it, their *healthy-ness*.

Please read this book with an open mind. The subject matter I am embarking on here has become highly controversial. Misinformation abounds, and the success stories are many times inflated, or perceived to be contrived. Again, I will encourage you to discuss any or all of what I'm sharing here with your physician and/or other medical professionals you know and trust. Perhaps sharing a copy of this book with them will make a difference for many people, now and in the years to come.

My life experience, along with my journey to drop over a hundred pounds is a raw one that exposes my vulnerabilities. The village of people whom I have surrounded myself with is comprised of real people. You can change your life from the inside out using some of what I'm sharing with you here, and that is as real as anything else in your life right now. Let's explore together, and know that I am sharing this story with you because I care about it so deeply.

CHAPTER ONE

A Brief History of Intermittent Fasting

"There is nothing new, except what's been forgotten.

~ Marie Antoinette

Intermittent fasting is not new. It is truly an idea that has withstood the test of time. In fact, the three most influential people to have ever lived have all agreed that fasting is a beneficial process. If this was a harmful practice, do you not think we would have figured this out, oh, say 1000 years ago?

Fasting for spiritual purposes is widely practiced, and remains part of virtually every major religion in the world. Jesus Christ, Buddha and the prophet Muhammed all shared a common belief in the healing power of fasting. The Church of Jesus Christ of Latter Day Saints teaches the Word of Wisdom, where the enlightened are instructed on how, what, and when to eat and when to fast. In spiritual terms, it is often called cleansing or purification, but practically, it amounts to the same thing.

Cave people did not eat all day long, or celebrate happy occasions with food. Grazing, the act of eating small amounts of high-calorie and less than nutritious foods is a modern-day habit.

Also, fasting in various forms is one of the most ancient and widespread healing traditions in the world. Hippocrates is widely

7

considered the father of modern medicine. Among the treatments that he prescribed and championed was the practice of fasting, and the consumption of apple cider vinegar as a natural appetite suppressant.

Hippocrates wrote, "To eat when you are sick, is to feed your illness." The ancient Greek writer and historian Plutarch shared these sentiments and wrote, "Instead of using medicine, better fast today." Ancient Greek thinkers Plato and his student Aristotle were also staunch supporters of fasting.

If this was a harmful practice, or one that led to negative consequences I believe human beings would have figured this out at least a thousand, or even more years ago. Intermittent fasting has become shrouded in controversy. This is a good thing, as it brings more attention to the topic of weight loss and helps to educate more people, based on my opinions and personal experience.

Dr. Jason Fung is currently one of the leading experts in this area. He recently said,

"All foods will increase insulin levels to some degree. Eating the proper foods will prevent high levels, but won't do much to lower levels. Some foods are better than others, but all foods still increase insulin. The key to prevention of resistance is to periodically sustain very low levels of insulin. If all foods raise insulin, then the only answer is the complete voluntary abstinence of food."

Fung added, "So, the forgotten question of weight loss is "When should we eat?" We don't ignore the question of frequency anywhere else. Falling from a building 1000 feet off the ground once will likely kill us. But is this the same as falling from a 1-foot wall 1000 times? Absolutely not. Yet the total distance fallen is still 1000 feet. The answer we are looking for is, in a word, fasting."

Then there is Johns Hopkins neuroscientist Mark Mattson, Ph.D., who has studied intermittent fasting for more than 25 years. He says that our bodies have evolved to be able to go without food for many hours, or even several days or longer. In prehistoric times, before humans learned to farm, they were hunters and gatherers who evolved to survive, and thrive for long periods without eating. They had to: It took a lot of time and energy to hunt game and gather nuts and berries.

Even 50 years ago, it was easier to maintain a healthy weight. Johns' Hopkins dietitian Christie Williams, M.S., R.D.N., explains: "There were no computers, and TV shows turned off at 11 p.m.; people stopped eating because they went to bed. Portions were much smaller. More people worked and played outside and, in general, got more exercise.

Nowadays, TV, the internet and other entertainment are available 24/7. We stay awake for longer hours to catch our favorite shows, play games and chat online. We're sitting and snacking all day — and most of the night."

Extra calories and less activity can mean a higher risk of obesity, type 2 diabetes, high blood pressure, arthritis, heart disease and a variety of other illnesses, maladies, and issues. Scientific studies are showing that intermittent fasting may help reverse these trends.

Please remember that this style of eating is a controversial one, and that my story is based on my personal experiences since beginning my ongoing journey in March of 2020.

How I Was Introduced to This Lifestyle

I don't believe I ever knew anyone who practiced IF (I'll use this as an abbreviation for intermittent fasting throughout this book), or at least I do not recall hearing anyone talk about it throughout my life. Then I began to hear about it a couple of years ago from two people I've known online and in person for over a decade, Dr. Ellen Britt, PA, Ed.D. and Denise Wakeman. Note: They each wrote a Foreword for this book that details their own experience and results, as well as the relationship I have with each of them.

I knew that Dr. Ellen had been a Physician Assistant for many years before I met her through my online business. I found out later that she had returned to school to earn her Ed.D. in Biology over the last several years. Denise was a serious runner and hiker and her trip to Machu Picchu made me long to be able to do something similar as a part of my own life experience. Both women are serious about health, wellness, anti-aging, and longevity and have taken their studies far beyond the hobby level.

Denise and Dr. Ellen announced their 10-Day Intermittent Fasting Challenge at the end of February, 2020. Coincidentally, Denise was to be one of my speakers the following week at the twice annual marketing conference I host in Los Angeles.

I registered for the 10-Day Challenge without giving it much thought. In my mind, this was insurance for the future, giving me permission to eat what I wanted and to visit the Starbucks across the street from the hotel each day during my conference. I liked my habit of saving up my bonus rewards and treating my guests to anything they wanted. It had become a ritual over the years that we all looked forward to throughout our days together.

Also, I believed that having Denise there that weekend would allow me to ask her questions about IF. I had recommended the Challenge to the people in attendance and quite a few had signed up. Interestingly enough, few questions were asked and I didn't even pay attention to what, or when Denise was eating that weekend.

The Challenge began on Monday, March 9th, 2021. By Friday, March 13th the United States had declared a State of Emergency due to the COVID-19 outbreak. By the time we completed the Challenge on Friday the 20th, the world was beginning to shut down.

Though I am not prone to depression, I honestly believed that this situation held the potential be harmful to my mental health. Over the weekend of March 21st and 22nd I made my plan to stay focused, productive, and sane for as many months as it would take for the effects of the virus outbreak to subside.

At the top of my list was intermittent fasting, and I knew that working closely with Dr. Ellen Britt, PA, Ed.D. and Denise Wakeman was an integral part of my plan. At the end of the 10-Day Challenge I came aboard for their ongoing Fast Factor group that has now become a very important part of my daily life.

Why Intermittent Fasting is So Effective

In my personal experience, I have found IF to be effective for two simple reasons; it's easy to understand and get started as a way of eating and it's effective and can show some results within a few weeks.

In my case, it took me almost a full month before I became what is referred to as "fat adapted" (more on this here and later) and began to drop some weight. Then, I took off and have never looked back.

The concept of fat adaptation refers to your body's ability to convert fat into energy. When you are fat-adapted, you don't need a steady stream of carbs (glucose) to fuel your day. Instead, you tap into a more abundant energy supply - your body fat.

Fat-adapted just means you can easily access fat (either dietary fat or body fat) for energy. It doesn't mean that glucose can't or won't get burned. And so having carbs now and then - provided it's not an excessive amount is no problem for the fat-adapted enthusiast.

Getting Started with Intermittent Fasting

I wanted to get started with this new way of eating slowly. Instead of diving in head first with rose colored goggles, I decided to tiptoe into the shallow end of the pool and see how it felt to my ankles and toes. This proved to be an excellent strategy for me. By giving myself the time to adapt to the new ideas and information I was receiving, I believe this increased my chances for success.

It took the first full week of the 10-Day Challenge for me to decide *when* I would eat each day. As is often the case when you are new to something, your perceptions are not the reality. I had previously believed that IF would require me to go without eating or drinking anything (other than plain water) for a full day or even longer, and on a regular basis. This is not true, but is a choice, and is one of the mistaken beliefs around this lifestyle.

Though there are people who advocate such a plan with this method, Dr. Ellen and Denise did not take this tack with what they were sharing with me and others in the group during the Challenge. Instead, we were asked to choose a period of time each day where we would "feast," and the remainder of the day would be our "fast."

I chose to begin with a 14:10, meaning that I fasted during a fourteen-hour period each day and feasted for ten hours. Keeping in mind that I'd be asleep for at least seven of those fourteen "fasting" hours made it sound more doable for me.

I will note here that many people begin with a 12:12 fast. This is certainly an acceptable way of easing into the idea of limiting the number of hours where you consume food each day. In fact, the young woman I began coaching, soon after receiving my Intermittent Fasting Coach Certification told me that twelve hours a day was too many for her and started with a 14:10 of her own volition. After a couple of weeks, I had a discussion with her and explained that while this schedule would improve her health, it might not be enough hours of fasting each day for her to drop much, if any weight.

I was used to eating almost immediately after rising each day and not stopping until an hour or so before going to bed. This was because I thought I had an issue with low blood sugar and not eating first thing in the morning would lead to headaches, loss of clarity, and an irritable mood that others did not want to be in the same room with. So, my first week of intermittent fasting consisted of eating from seven in the morning until five in the afternoon.

Also, I was not a coffee or tea drinker, and the thought of black coffee or green or black tea without milk, cream, sugar, or other sweeteners was not exactly appealing to me.

But I was determined to give this style of eating a chance, so I approached what they were sharing with me with an open mind. There were people I knew in the group they had set up for us on Facebook, and many more I did not know. Some of the stories resonated with me, others did not, and several people seemed to have had a similar life experience as to what I had been living.

The second week I got back on the scale and still hadn't lost one pound. But this did not deter me, as I forced myself to look at the much larger picture of being able to become fat-adapted, eat a little healthier than I was used to for over a decade, and feeling better about my health and my future than I had in decades.

Up until this time, I had been a quitter and someone who did not follow through unless I could see tangible evidence that something would work for me. But I had faith in the process and in Denise and Dr. Ellen to guide me along the path to success. I'm so glad I made this decision, as it has changed my life, as well as saving my life because of my health status at the beginning of my journey.

There was also a tease from Dr. Ellen at some point that second week that intrigued me to no end. She mentioned that intermittent fasting was effective for the anti-aging benefits that were possible, namely through something called autophagy.

If for no other reason, I believed that the state of autophagy was worth working towards. Keeping in mind that I am not an expert in this area and have absolutely no medical experience, this is how I can describe autophagy to you…

Autophagy comes from the Greek and breaks down to *auto*, meaning self, and *phagy*, which means to eat, making the process of autophagy one in which the human body devours itself.

As morbid as that may sound, it is actually a wondrous thing to be able to slough off old, worn out cells in favor of new, energetic ones. We're accustomed to this when we brush or wash our hair, shower, and exfoliate. Who knew that we could do this for our organs and body systems, and set it all on autopilot?

It Takes a Village

Very little in life is accomplished on our own. Instead, our achievements are the product of the village we have created for ourselves. This village consists of the people and resources we assemble in order to achieve the goals we have in mind.

For example, as I was out for my morning walk this morning, I passed by a house where a family with five very little children used to live. I now live in two different cities simultaneously, so I'm not as aware of who is living a few blocks away from my first house as I was years ago.

I believe there was at least one set of toddler twins and the oldest was about five years old, in my memory. A man was coming out of the house as I walked by, and I stopped to asked him if he knew what had happened to that family.

As we were speaking, the front door opened and out stepped a beautiful young lady. The man pointed and said, "This is the youngest. They're all teenagers now, driving and working at part-time jobs. I know you may not recognize me, but I'm the dad of those five little children you remember."

We laughed and talked some more, and he thanked me for some books I have given to his children all those years ago. "Thank you for your help with this," he added. By "this" he was referring to the concept that many people help raise a child, and it takes a village to make it all happen.

My recommendation is that you begin to assemble your own "village" if you have the intention of improving your health overall, working on a specific area of your health that is an issue for you, or lose a significant amount of weight.

This village will include people that will support you physically, intellectually, and emotionally along your journey, including doctors and other medical professionals, experts and specialists in the areas where you need help, and people who may be your friends, family members, neighbors, co-workers, colleagues, clergy, and anyone else you feel the need to include.

My village in regards to my health consists of a number of people. This includes Dr. Ellen Britt, PA, Ed.D. and Denise Wakeman guiding me specifically with my journey, as well as Dr. Bassem El Tom, my personal physician who is monitoring my progress from strictly a medical, although highly human perspective.

I also include in my health and wellness village Cheryl A. Major, CNWC (Certified Nutrition and Wellness Consultant) as someone who helped me to change my thinking about what was possible for me. For over a decade, she has guided me to make better food choices and taught me a new way of thinking about food and the relationship I have with it.

For a number of years, Cheryl and I have roomed together when she comes to California for my marketing events. I live driving distance from the hotel where I host these events, so I typically bring tableware, flatware, and some food items with me. Then we visit local markets to purchase the food items we need during our stay.

Cheryl puts together delicious, healthy, and nutritious breakfasts and lunches for us, and I clean up and do the dishes. It's a match made in the healthy part of Heaven on Earth! We eat dinner with the other attendees to socialize and share the days' topics with one another. Over the years, the conversation has naturally moved to food and eating because of the emphasis Cheryl makes in this area of her life and business with people all over the world.

Along with the foods I choose to eat, my body needs to move each day. Kathy Denise Hicks came into my life in April of 2020, just a month after I began my IF practice. With her guidance and daily workout routines, my body is now in motion in a way that serves me. Her decades of experience with fitness and exercise continue to make sense for the goals I've set for myself. While I will never be an athlete, working with Kathy makes me feel like one, at least at the amateur level.

Also, search for resources that will make your village even stronger than it would be with only the people I just suggested. These resources will include books both in print and electronic format; magazines and other periodical publications; podcasts and other audio recordings; videos; any types of apps for your phone or tablet; and live or virtual events, courses, and programs.

If you included even one item from each of the categories I've mentioned here to the inventory available to you and the other people in your village, your life experience and specific results would be enhanced and enriched exponentially.

CHAPTER TWO

Food as Fuel

"Food, in the end, in our own tradition, is something holy. It's
not so much about nutrients and calories. It's about sharing,
honesty, and identity."

~ Louise Fresco

Let's go back in time, long before I discovered intermittent fasting.
Now we'll step back even further, to a point in time where I had
a handle on my weight and health and was at a good place in my life.
It was on Thursday, November 13, 1983, between eleven and eleven
fifteen that morning.

Of course, I am being silly here but the truth is that, except for a
month or two here and there I was always aware that my weight, and
the related health issues that ensued was definitely something I needed
to address and to deal with.

The Emotional Connection: Eating for Love and Acceptance

I grew up as the only child of a single mother, after my parents
separated when I was three years old. Life is very different with only
two people in the household, as you may already be aware of from your
own life experience or that of someone close to you.

But when you have one adult and one child the dynamics are
skewed in favor of what's the easiest to accomplish along the path of

least resistance. We both had emotional trauma related to our situation. I was not the easiest child for many reasons. So, my mother did the best she could under the circumstances and I am grateful to have had her by my side during those years while I was growing up.

My favorite foods as a child were mashed potatoes, anything containing chocolate, and white bread with butter slathered all over it. It was probably margarine or something called "bread spread" rather than butter, but I can't be sure because it was so long ago.

Potatoes were inexpensive and chocolate meant a five cent Hershey bar back then. I did eat other things, like frozen pot pies, macaroni and cheese, bologna sandwiches and hot dogs. The occasional banana and other fruits were mostly an afterthought.

My mother and I were what is now referred to as "food insecure" until I was in junior high. That coincided with me starting to earn some money with mowing lawns, babysitting, and performing odd jobs for people we knew in the neighborhood. One summer I scraped barnacles off a boat until my knuckles were bloody, but the pay was very good and the job lasted for several weeks.

But until I began bringing in some money to our household, buying food was a daily struggle. A hot lunch at school cost a quarter back then. Once a month, my mother would put five quarters in four envelopes to cover each day's lunch for the month. But as we needed the money for other necessities, the quarters slowly disappeared. And, there are almost always more than twenty school days during a calendar month.

Some days, I pretended I wasn't hungry and spent my lunchtime in the library at school. Or, I would feign illness and lie down in the nurse's office where they would prepare a glass of bicarbonate of soda to soothe my stomach. In either case, my behavior was setting up a pattern around food that was not healthy.

Once a month, on the day my mother received her paycheck we would take the bus downtown and treat ourselves like royalty. Yes, I would miss school that day. The school never commented on this self-imposed and implemented monthly day off because I was an excellent student and the world was very different at that time in history.

Occasionally, we would meet up with my mother's friend, Judy for lunch at a local eatery and then some shopping. Judy worked at the largest bank in downtown Miami at that time and loved spending time with us during her lunch hour.

After lunch, we would browse in Jordan Marsh or Burdine's. These were the largest department stores in the city and their downtown locations were spectacular to behold. Jordan Marsh had a cafeteria on the top floor that also had a bakery section. The brownies were my favorite and I would eat mine in three swift bites so there weren't any crumbs.

One day after our lunch together, we bought three brownies for us to eat in Bayfront Park. This gorgeous park faced Biscayne Bay and was both invigorating and serene. The main public library was located right there, along with interesting people and feral cats who lived beneath the library and were only friendly when begging for food from the passersby.

After walking a couple of blocks, we realized we had left our box of brownies on the counter at the bakery. Judy and my mother said they didn't care about them, but I insisted on running back to get them and then catching up with them at the park.

I ended up eating all three brownies before meeting up with them twenty minutes later. They didn't ask me where the box was, but they had to know what had happened. That was the first time I felt guilty about eating too much, especially with food that had little to no nutritional value, but it wouldn't be the last.

Now I understand that food is simply fuel for the body. We choose what, when, and how to eat based upon a number of things. Bringing together the foods we love with the knowledge and understanding that the right foods fuel us more effectively is a powerful concept and worth devoting our time and attention to each day, I believe. Just as we have a choice of which grade and octane of gasoline to purchase in order to fuel our automobile, we also have a choice when it comes to fueling our bodies.

The Emotional Connection with Food and Eating

Around this time, during the years while I was still in elementary school marked the beginning of my emotional relationship with food. Food was my friend. Food didn't care about the clothes I wore, the house I lived in, or the way I looked. When others hurt my feelings, food was there to soothe me and make me feel like everything was going to be alright.

On some level, I'm sure that my mother, the teachers at my school, and other adults who passed in and out of my life during those years knew that something was wrong. But during the 1960s and into the 70s people didn't talk about such personal and private things in the way they would these days.

The summer after elementary school, leading into the fall at the new junior high was a pivotal time for me. I wanted to wear the clothes my friends would be wearing and the only way to do that was to lose some weight. Dresses and skirts would make me look and feel more like the mature young lady I so desperately wanted to become.

I learned about calories, and the caloric value of each food and beverage I consumed. Let's spend a minute discussing some of what I'm referring to here…

A calorie is defined as the energy needed to raise the temperature of 1 kilogram of water through 1 °C, equal to one thousand small calories and often used to measure the energy value of foods.

The amount of energy in an item of food or drink is measured in calories. When we eat and drink more calories than we use up, our bodies store the excess as body fat. A calorie is a unit of energy. When you hear something contains 100 calories, it's a way of describing how much energy your body could get from eating or drinking it.

The game of tennis had become important to me that summer, and I practiced hitting the ball against the back wall of a store down the street to perfect my two-handed serve. I had learned this from studying the reigning super star of tennis at the time, Chris Everett and then gained the confidence needed to play against more experienced players.

This made me feel better about myself than ever before in my memory, and the weight came off as I continued my daily regimen of no more than five hundred calories and at least two hours of tennis practice.

I entered the 7th grade a Horace Mann Junior High the Tuesday after Labor Day in 1967. Six elementary schools fed into this school and we had over a thousand students in grades seven through nine.

A few people knew me from elementary school, but most of them didn't recognize me. The other students were meeting me for the first time. For once in my life, I fit in. In fact, if the first week was any indication of what was to come, I had the potential to become one of the cool kids for a change.

I learned a lot more than the six subjects on my schedule that fall. By the end of October, I had gained back the twenty pounds I had lost, and then some. Little did I know at that time that I was not only entering the awkward teen years, but also about to engage in more than a decade of ups and downs, related to my emotions, my physical health, and more.

To this day, my emotional state affects the foods I choose to eat and the span of time I will eat them during any given day. My goal is to check in with myself regularly, throughout each day to make sure I feel happy, strong, confident, and empowered by my food choices. Once I took full responsibility for all of my actions, along with the results that followed, I began the process of reinventing my life. This is an empowering feeling I want you to have as well.

Eating for Control

Consuming food can be a complicated process. I'm not talking about choosing the specific foods we will eat, or shopping for or preparing food. I am referring to food as a passive-aggressive tactic in order to control a situation.

Children learn this at a very young age. We've all been around a toddler or preschooler who refused to eat as a way to control the adults in their life. Food represents power and position, especially when you have very little of that in your life otherwise.

What we eat and don't eat can bring us attention from the people close to us. If we seek approval from someone around us, eating the foods they do is sure to be the place to begin. Refusing to eat something someone has prepared for us can bring out feelings and actions we couldn't have anticipated.

Food is at the center of our social lives. We celebrate with food. We mourn with food. We connect with others through shared culinary experiences. Without food, our common denominator shifts to something different, and perhaps more evolved. Food can define us in a way that works both for and against our goals and intentions.

I'll talk about this topic in greater detail later on. For now, think about your eating habits and patterns and how they are serving you in ways that go far beyond simply fueling your body.

Let's revisit junior high, as I share my "yo-yo" and teen years story and experience…

CHAPTER 3

The Yo-Yo Years

"Unity is strength. Where there is teamwork and collaboration, wonderful things can be achieved."

~ Mattie Stepanek

In the previous chapter, I joked about the famous twenty minutes where I was in control of my health. Now, let's go back in time, before I discovered intermittent fasting. For the moment, we'll step back even further, to a point in time where I had a handle on my weight and health and was at a good place psychologically in my life.

The truth is that except for a month or two here and there, I have been aware that my weight was an issue since I was in elementary school. Then I culminated from the 6th grade and spent the summer worrying about how I would fit in with the other kids when I entered the new school in the fall. I set about to find a diet that I could stick with to lose some weight before the leaves began to drop from the trees and the temperatures cooled down.

Junior high isn't an easy place to maneuver under the best of circumstances. But added to the already stressful situation was the fact that I was the largest person in my homeroom. This was despite the fact that I had lost weight – about twenty pounds – before school had begun.

I know this because my homeroom teacher, Mrs. Cline took me

aside on the first day and asked me if I needed a "sturdier" chair. This was the politically correct way to make me feel more comfortable at my desk for the thirty minutes I would spend in her Homeroom each morning. I declined her invitation and instead resorted to finding creative ways to be out of my seat as much of the time as possible.

I took the attendance report to the office, checked my locker, went to the bathroom, and sauntered in and out of her classroom, enjoying Homeroom immensely.

Then Patrick arrived at school. He was the cutest boy I'd ever encountered and I liked him right away. Perhaps I reminded him of his sister or another girl in his life, because he liked me as well. But not in *that* way. Instead, I was doomed to be in the "friend zone" all semester and destined for loneliness and almost no acceptance from others for romantic encounters, innocent as they would be at that age.

Instinctively, I believed that one semester would turn into a year or longer, and that this boy was only the first of a lifetime of not being accepted by the opposite sex.

One day, I asked my new friend Gigi to ask Patrick if he liked me. Boys can be brutally honest and he told her he liked me as a friend because I was "too big in all the wrong places." I brushed it off when she delivered the news, but it was symbolic, and the beginning of what was to come.

The In Between Teen Years

As anyone who knew me personally back then could have predicted, junior high led to high school and my issues around weight grew. Literally. The only other girl bigger than me was a girl named Cookie. It was a nickname, but she insisted on keeping it and suffered through the teasing by the other kids who thrived at coming up with ever more creative and cruel ways to incorporate her name into a joke.

I longed to be more like a girl named Kathy. She was the prettiest girl in all of our junior high school. Almost weekly, she would announce that she had broken up with one boy and was now going steady with another. She was our school's version of the femme fatale who had her way with any boy who was brave or foolhardy enough to approach her with romantic intentions. But down deep she was sweet and kind and finding her way as well.

Luckily for me, I was not the stereotype of either of these girls, but somewhere in between. I settled for being known as the funny girl who could make everyone laugh. I was so sensitive, and the humor covered it nicely. This, along with my newfound quest for being known as one of the smart kids saved me from all kinds of ill fate during those years.

Fad Diets

Most people are not very patient, I have discovered. Between the ages of twelve and eighteen, I refused to even spell that word correctly. I wanted to lose weight and there was no time to waste. That's when I learned about so-called "fad" diets that promised quick results, without mentioning how they could affect the human body.

The weirdest one was the "apple diet" where you could eat as many apples as you wanted for three days. No other foods or beverages were permitted. My stomach was in knots and I did lose weight as a result, though most of it returned within a couple of days. I decided to do this every week and eat regular food during the remaining four days of each week.

This led to a variety of maladies, including digestive issues related to eating too much fiber, embarrassing flatulence, fluctuations in blood sugar, and an excessive consumption of dangerous, cancer-causing pesticides.

Up, Down, and All Around

My weight went up and down like a ship on a stormy sea. My closet was arranged and organized into three sections: On the left were the clothes that fit me right now. In the middle I hung the clothes that had fit me at one time, but not any longer. And on the right side of my closet there were two pairs of pants that I loved but had never fit me, along with two dresses and a jacket I had never been able to wear.

If you aren't familiar with the term *honesty pants*, I will share that this refers to a pair of pants, or other piece of clothing that lets us know when we have gained a few pounds and need to slow down our eating and step up our exercising. I've owned dozens of these throughout my lifetime, but those days are over now. Here is an article I penned about my experiences with this topic…

Honesty Pants

The honesty pants started out as an impulse purchase from Macy's on lower State Street. I had originally thought they were black but when I attempted to squeeze into them at home the next day, I realized they were sort of an olive green. My first thought was that I had the perfect blouse to go with that color, but as I pulled them up over my knees I knew that I might never fit into these pants. The honest truth was that I knew they were too small when I took them off the rack and held them up so the light coming through the skylight above would help me decide if I wanted them or not. I wanted them. They were on the second markdown, making them even more appealing. Now I just wanted them to fit me, and once they did to never grow too large for them again.

Finding clothes to fit me had been the issue since I started Kindergarten. I wanted a plaid jumper but the saleslady told my mother that line stopped at 6X. That's when you have to go to regular girl's sizes and the choices aren't nearly as cute. So, we brought it home anyway and if memory serves my mother stopped making mashed potatoes filled with more margarine than potato and macaroni and cheese that was more cheese than macaroni. On the first day of school the jumper fit like a glove. That made me happy, which in turn made my mother smile.

At recess I climbed to the top of the jungle gym and proclaimed myself to be "Queen of the Whole School." When my subjects failed to stop in their tracks and give me the respect I was commanding I quickly jumped down, splitting the jumper right down the seam in the process. Before I could react one of the teachers took my hand and brought me into the classroom where she used the largest safety pins I had ever seen to put me back together so well no one else even noticed.

That marked the end of my innocence and after that day we shopped in the girl's section of the store for my clothes.

As a child I was impatient and lacked focus. If you are familiar with the "Marshmallow Test" where young children are given the option of eating one marshmallow now or waiting for five minutes to have two marshmallows, I would have definitely been in the group that wanted mine immediately. I did not understand the concept of delayed gratification until much later in life.

I was pretty much unaware of my body until the sixth grade. That was when Michael Shiffrin came into my life and I fell in love in the cafeteria line. His wavy brown hair and deep like the ocean green eyes mesmerized me from the moment we met. Michael only had eyes for Debbie Howard, a popular blond who was always very nice to me. One day I raised my hand to ask Mrs. Nairn if I could use the restroom, and on my way down the open hallway I saw Michael and Debbie talking by the drinking fountain. Debbie smiled and I walked closer to them but Michael ignored me. He even kept his hand on the faucet so I couldn't get a drink. As I was walking away, I turned slightly to see him with his cheeks puffed out. Debbie was not smiling.

Darting into the girl's bathroom I felt my face, hot and red. Michael had been making fun of me. By filling his cheeks with air, he was insinuating that I was fat. I looked in the bathroom mirror and did a quick appraisal of my appearance. I was fat. In that moment Michael did not seem so dreamy and I lost confidence in my worth as a human being.

Two years later I was sitting next to Patrick Tanasi in Mrs. Cline's homeroom. Pat was handsome and funny and charming and I liked him so much. One day we walked together to our respective first period classes and he stopped at his locker while I kept going. My friend Gigi came up behind me, winded and smiling from ear to ear.

"Patrick just asked me to the dance. I'm so excited!" she announced.

I don't remember if I answered her but the message came through loud and clear; I was Patrick's friend but would never be his girlfriend. I vowed to go on a diet and to never go steady with him, even if he begged me. I was now equating popularity with looks, a pattern that would last for decades.

My time as a yo-yo dieter took its toll on my health, both mental and physical. It was my belief that when I could manage to keep my weight down that more people, guys and girls alike, wanted to be my friend. This was proven to be true when Stephen asked me out and soon after asked me to be his girlfriend. Now I was one of the popular girls and my life would be filled with fun and excitement and love.

The longer Stephen and I dated the more confident I became. We had many friends, including couples we could double date with on the weekends. I was on top of the world or so I thought. He said he loved me and I believed it was unconditional.

That summer we both took part-time jobs. He was a lifeguard at our local pool; I was a waitress at the IHOP. He grew taller and stronger and more fit while I ate too much and was too tired to ride my bicycle with him after work each evening.

When he broke up with me, he said things that hurt me very deeply. He wanted to be with someone who liked more of the things he liked, who would understand when he wanted to be with the guys, who was… someone else. He wanted someone thinner and prettier and that was someone else than me.

I was crushed at this loss and began a period of grieving that lasted into the fall and winter that year and into the next. I had never experienced a loss of this magnitude and didn't want to share my feelings with anyone. I was in shock and unable to snap myself out of it. It was as if someone had died, and deep inside I knew that might be me and I would never recover.

Said author Joan Didion, after experiencing the death of her husband, "Grief turns out to be a place none of us know until we reach it. We anticipate (we know) that someone close to us could die, but we do not look beyond the few days or weeks that immediately follow such an imagined death. We misconstrue the nature of even those few days or weeks. We might expect if the death is sudden to feel shock. We do not expect the shock to be obliterative, dislocating to both body and mind."

As an adult I learned how to diet effectively. This meant starving myself until I could once again fit into the clothes I wanted to wear. Fad diets were predominant, including the "apple" diet where you only ate apples, but you could eat as many as you wanted to and any type of apple was acceptable. The easiest one for me was to count calories and only allow myself five hundred a day. I would lose a pound a day by sticking to this and I can remember one time after doing it for a month gorging myself on buttermilk pancakes at the local restaurant that had an "all you can eat" breakfast deal one Sunday a month.

I had a clothing size – size 12 – that I would not go beyond, yet I dreamed of being a size 8. It still amazes me that people all over the world can become obsessed with wearing a specific size of clothing. The truth is that different designers and clothing companies set the standard measurements for clothing.

During the times when my weight wasn't an issue all was right in the world. I based everything I did on how I looked and forgot about how I felt. Stuffing my feelings replaced stuffing my face and the only thing that mattered was how I looked on the outside. My jobs and relationships and life achievements were measured in pounds and inches and clothing sizes, instead of on deeper ideas and loftier aspirations. Younger bodies respond more easily to fad diets and neglect and excesses but I believed that someday it would all be different. Someday I would be able to maintain my goal weight without having to think about it. Someday I would marry a man who would love me no matter what I looked like or how much I weighed. And someday my life would be exactly how I had dreamed it should be. Someday...

There was always next month, next summer, next year to get to my goal weight and clothing size. When you're young, you are convinced you have all the time in the world to do those things you keep saying you truly want to do. Then the time passes and life happens and one day you're three bills and change and the doctor prescribes four different drugs to bring down the blood pressure and to stave off diabetes. He skips the lecture because he has given up and when you ask if losing weight could take it all back and make it go away, he nods and looks past me, not uttering a word as he backs out of the exam room.

And then you sit in the car outside of the pharmacy and cry until you can taste the salt from your tears and you ask yourself where the time went and why you didn't get it together sooner. But no answers come and you resign yourself to the fact that everyone else will have the life they want and the relationships, and the clothes, and the vacations and the fun and the...

The text message is from the pharmacy and my prescriptions are ready. There's a glucose monitor and lancets and more pills than I have ever seen with my name on them. They ask if I have questions but I can't think of any and I drive home the long way. I go past the lake where I have dreamed of walking with friends but didn't have the energy to do more than sit on the bench and take pictures of the ducks and geese and turtles. I drive by the elementary school and think back to my twenty years of teaching, measured by how much I weighed and how I would be accepted by others. There were a few "fat years" that were okay. The children accepted me for who I was on the outside but I didn't trust that this was what I should have expected from everyone in my life. I can only think of two years when I was at a healthy weight and now, I can't think of how they were better than the others. Perhaps they were all the same.

My life has been a series of ups and downs and numbers that get larger and smaller and disappointments, in myself mostly and now it might be too late, no, it's never too late and when I return home, I take a long nap to dream of a way to solve my dilemma. Instead, I toss and turn going over the questions I can't answer. I need to do something, but what? I need help, but what would that look like? I need a plan, but my experience with plans related to dieting have not been successful. I need something else.

When I get out of bed because sleep did not come on that day I go through my photos on iCloud. I go back to 2017 when my extended family visited me in California from their native Finland for a month. We all look so happy, excited to be together in so many wonderful places. Then I fixate on a series of photos taken at Disneyland during our three days in the happiest place on Earth. The emotions come as I recall the day in California Adventure where we waited in line for the Radiator Springs ride. It had been one of the highlights of their previous trip two years earlier and something we had talked about for months.

As we got closer to the front of the line my stepdaughter and I looked at each other while thinking the same thing. Would we be able to fit in the seats this time? After several attempts we excused ourselves and the two cars holding our family left the station. We consoled ourselves with ice cream and talked about how next time it would be different for us. But would we really lose the weight and keep it off the next time? The tears flow and I think about the example I am not setting for the rest of the family, the children I did not influence to eat better and exercise during my twenty years of classroom teaching, and the damage I am doing to my body, not to mention the psychological implications of feeling the way I do each day because of something I could take control of and change.

Now I'm standing in my closet, a room larger than any I ever had as a bedroom while growing up. Today I must try on the honesty pants to see if I will be able to wear them in just less than three weeks to my live, in person event I am hosting in Los Angeles. It's the third week of February, 2020 and I want this event to be a special one. Even if the pants are too tight, I will have enough time to lose a few pounds to squeeze into them, at least for a few hours during the first day. The honesty on this day will be one more painful reminder of who I am and what I intend to do, someday.

I take the pants carefully off the hanger and hold them up to the light, much as I did when I bought them just before last Christmas. I hold my breath and cross my fingers and slowly step into them. I know by the time I have both feet and lower legs in they are not even close to fitting me right now. The honesty is almost too much for me and I yank them off and leave them on the closet floor. Now I am calculating how many days and how many pounds and how many calories I can eat between today, February 14th — my God, is it really Valentine's Day today? — and the day I will drive into Los Angeles to the hotel. Yes, it's possible.

Possible, but not probable. My behavior has become predictable and as each day begins and I promise I will start my diet that day I know down deep that by noon I will have an excuse for not getting started. Then I begin to beat myself up. My argument since I started my business in 2006 has been that if I am capable of succeeding as an author and entrepreneur and public speaker, I most certainly should be able to successfully lose weight and keep it off. I have what I refer to as "crossover skills" that should transfer over from one part of my life to another. This just hasn't been the case so far, but it's coming someday soon.

I check my email and see the message from Denise Wakeman about the intermittent fasting challenge she is hosting with her business partner, Dr. Ellen Britt, P.A, Ed.D. I've known both of them for more than a decade yet I know little about this part of their lives. Denise will be speaking at my event again this year and the challenge begins the day after we finish. Yes, I will sign up and be able to talk to her about it while we are together in Los Angeles.

The world begins to unravel during the following week and I am about to come apart at the seams wondering what this will look like in the coming weeks. The virus we first heard about in January has now reached the United States. I call the hotel almost every day and hold my breath as they give me the latest update. No one has cancelled and they will be full while I am there. They aren't sure what would happen if I wanted to cancel. Do I want to cancel? No, if even one person from my group shows up, I will be there for all five days, I reassure the event coordinator. I give only a passing thought to Denise and Dr. Ellen and the intermittent fasting challenge, except to note that I can eat what I want right now because it won't begin until Monday, March 9th, the day after my event ends. I hang up the honesty pants on a velvet lined hangar, draping the blouse that will match them over the top to keep the outfit together.

By divine intervention we are able to have the event during the very last weekend it would have been possible. A two-hundred-person wedding party cancels for Saturday. The flight crews that regularly stay at this hotel because of its close proximity to LAX begin checking out in mass as flights are cancelled and they are sent home. By the end of the weekend my group is the only one still at the hotel and we are beginning to realize that things are changing at a faster pace now. As I drive home on the eerily quiet freeway I think about the challenge and I am excited to begin the next morning.

Intermittent fasting has not only changed, but is saving my life. My doctor is over the moon with my ongoing, steady progress and believes me when I say this way of eating will serve me forever. And, as for the olive-green honesty pants with the matching floral print blouse? The outfit fits me, not like a glove but comfortably and I only feel bad knowing that someday soon they will be too large for me to wear. Then I will preserve them for eternity and tell my grandchildren the story when they are old enough to understand the meaning. Someday is coming soon and I am ready to embrace all that will mean in my life

.

SECTION 2

WHY HEALTH MUST BE A PRIORITY...
MY JOURNEY BEGINS

"Hope is being able to see that there is light, despite all of the darkness."

~ Desmond Tutu

After we know and understand what something *is*, we must then know *why* it is important. Intermittent fasting is a way of eating that includes a window of time in which we feast, then followed by a longer period of time when we fast.

I mentioned in the first chapter that I began my IF practice with a 14:10, meaning that I started limiting my eating window, or feast to no more than ten hours each day. This would lead into my fast, which lasted for fourteen hours and included the seven or so hours I was asleep each evening.

After about a month of maintaining this schedule, I shortened my feasting window, first to eight hours a day and finally to a six-hour period of eating. Whereas I had previously believed that I couldn't possibly go for so long without eating each day, I was pleasantly surprised to discover that my body found this new schedule quite agreeable and did not rebel against it in any way.

The weight began to come off and my energy and stamina increased to the point that it was noticeable by those around me in my daily life.

The next step would be to lower my A1C, the measure of my blood sugar used to determine diabetes. My new doctor had already begun ordering bottles of pills for me, along with a glucose monitor and other accessories. I was determined to turn this situation around and believed that maintaining my intermittent fasting challenge would be the key to improved health and a fresh start towards living the life I wanted and deserved.

I was able to achieve this goal, even though it sounded like a lofty one at the time and one that might not be possible. But with Dr. El Tom in my corner, along with Denise and Dr. Ellen I had faith that I was about to reinvent myself and change my life forever.

Our health must become a top priority throughout our lifetime. Even though I had health issues in my younger years, once I turned sixty I was aware that my body was beginning to slow down. I did not want to live this way. I was reminded of people I knew who walked more slowly and thoughtfully because they had accepted as a fact the idea that an advancing age meant slower and more difficult movement.

Once I began my eating and movement strategies around intermittent fasting, my body and mind shifted into high gear to serve and reward my newfound behavior.

I became a student of health and healthy living. This is when I began learning about Blue Zones, geographical areas throughout the world where the people are known to live well past the ages we assume would be at the upper limit of a human's lifespan.

CHAPTER 4

⊖✕⊖

Surrendering

"In order to reach our full potential, we must first be willing to humble ourselves to the people and situations which will move us forward."

~ Connie Ragen Green

This morning while I was walking, I realized that most of the people I encounter during this time of day – early mornings, before eight o'clock - are oblivious to the outside world. When someone does take the time to stop, remove as least one earbud, and speak with me, I always ask them why they're doing what they do.

The answers vary, but the idea is the same. They believe they are successfully multitasking by listening to music, a podcast, or an audio recording while they walk. Some say they use this time to speak on the phone with someone. And the ones who think about their answer tell me they hate to exercise and will do just about anything to make the time pass quickly so they can get back to what's truly important in their life. I worry they are missing the point completely, and also that they may not be able to hear a vehicle approaching or something else that could be an obstacle in their path.

Each morning I walk for at least an hour. This is my time to reflect, renew, and reinvent. It's the level of self-care I now wish to achieve throughout my day every single day, and it begins with the stretching and gentle walking that leads into my hiking practice.

My walking was a habit I'd had for years, yet I'd stopped completely during my first few years as an online entrepreneur.

The story I told myself was that I no longer had the time to do this, and that instead I needed to be in front of the computer every waking moment. Within the first month I had let my gym membership lapse. The second month found me returning to poor eating habits that included way too much refined sugar and carbohydrates and too much food altogether. By the third month the unwanted pounds had begun to return and my clothes were too tight. I tossed the "honesty pants" I wrote about here in a previous chapter as far into the back of the closet as possible and wouldn't give them another thought for several years.

It's About So Much More than Weight

Gaining weight is simply a symptom and side effect of something much bigger. It begins, I believe, in the recesses of your mind. It can start with one thought or idea, a harmless comment from outside influences, or even through the media, with social media playing a starring role.

We are social beings, even if we identify as being shy, or introverts, or even antisocial in some situations. The idea and concept of fitting in with others is always in the back of our minds. It's been shown that people will go to extremes, sometimes dangerous and unhealthy ones in order to be accepted by their peers.

I had joined Rotary, an international service organization soon after starting my online business and moving to a new city. At age 50, I was one of the younger members of the group, and looking back now I realize that I settled into the role of someone much older.

Every week we met for lunch at the Marie Callender's restaurant (known for their delicious pies and comfort food) in this new community. As I looked around at the other members, a part of me believed that my younger days were gone and that a life of service to others, both locally and throughout the world did not require me to be thin and in excellent physical shape in order for me to fit in.

The comfort foods and slice of pie I ordered each week soothed me. These people were willing to embrace me as the newest member, offer me friendship along with business advice, and include me in things I had not ever experienced before. With every project I slipped deeper into a false sense of security and reality. As 2006 slid into 2007, my weight went above two hundred pounds for the first time in many years. My way of addressing this was to purchase some new clothing that included pants with stretchy waistbands and darker colors. The next decade was more difficult for me in terms of health issues and injuries, and every bit of it was due to my own choices and actions.

Illness and Injury

Growing up as a healthy child and teenager, no one around me explained that being overweight is damaging to your overall level of health. I think perhaps it is seen as more of an emotional problem at the core and the effects of obesity are more of a personal nature than a medical one. This view is one that does not serve people, in my opinion.

Also, I came of age during the 1960s and 70s and there was a completely different mindset and belief system around what constituted optimal health during this time.

Our outward appearance is an important aspect of who we are, but it will always be what's on the inside that makes us the person we are. This usually refers to our heart and mind, and how we react and empathize with our fellow human beings. But there is also the health aspect and our insides include our organs and systems that keep us alive and healthy.

Diabetes, high blood pressure and even arthritis was only discussed in whispers and details were not readily available before the advent of the internet. We had a neighbor with what was then referred to as "sugar diabetes' when I was ten or eleven, but I mistakenly assumed that meant she was allergic to sugar and eating it would make her sick.

In my thirties I experienced an issue with my kidneys. Medication got me back to normal within about six months. During that time, I do not recall the doctors, other medical personnel, or anyone in my personal life discussing the role my diet and exercise had in my overall health. Medical schools offer very little training in the area of nutrition, and drugs and surgery are the usual remedies for most things that occur in our bodies and need medical attention.

This is backwards thinking, in my opinion. Why can't we teach people how to care for their bodies so they will run like a finely tuned piece of machinery? Instead, we wait until someone is ill and then prescribe drugs, some of which can be very dangerous to our overall health, and then move on to surgeries and other invasive procedures.

At age thirty-seven I was diagnosed with Stage 3 breast cancer. I'm a bit of a hypochondriac and had sought out medical attention after having what I thought was the flu during the previous several weeks.

When three doctors all told me they believed I had cancer, I went for additional blood work and an ultrasound. Within days, I was scheduled for a radical mastectomy and follow up with both chemotherapy and radiation.

At the time, I had been eating well, eliminating sugar almost entirely and adding more fruits and vegetables to my diet. Additionally, I had cut down my read meat consumption to no more than once a week and replaced it with fish and legumes. I was at a healthy weight, exercising regularly and feeling positive about my life at that time.

The day before the surgery, I decided to drive through McDonald's for my final meal. I'm not a fast-food enthusiast normally, but I was feeling like everything I had been doing to live a healthier lifestyle had backfired with this diagnosis. Just the smell of it reminded me that it was going against my inner feelings and beliefs to consume these items. When the sack was pushed through the window to me, it reeked of rancid cooking oil. The food was so greasy I didn't finish it and it even brought on a headache later that evening.

Throughout my cancer treatment, no one mentioned diet or exercise to me. When you're trying to save your life by following the advice of medical experts, you expect them to share everything that could be important. Their absence of information in this area led me to believe it wasn't so important, and that eating well, working out regularly, and maintaining a healthy weight was more of an exercise in vanity than anything else.

Obviously, I survived that bout with cancer. But the damage I was doing to my body with the types of food I was eating, the sheer amount I was consuming, along with my sedentary lifestyle would serve to scaffold my unhealthy habits into a mountain of illness and disease over time.

During the summer and into the fall of 2019 my A1C, the measure of your average blood sugar levels over the past three months, began to rise to unacceptable levels. The A1C test is one of the commonly used tests to diagnose prediabetes and diabetes, and is also the main test to help you and your health care team manage your diabetes. By December I was given the diagnosis of being "prediabetic" and this label was added to my medical chart. This is pretty much your permanent record and seldom would this improve: My denial of the situation would ensure that.

I changed to a new doctor (my dear Dr. El Tom) in January of 2020 and he began prescribing medications for diabetes, as well as a glucose monitor and supplies. I picked up a large bag of items from my local pharmacy. I explained that I was not diabetic, only prediabetic as they rung up my order and thanked me for stopping by. I made space in my bathroom cabinet for everything and never looked at any of it again.

When I had first met this new doctor in person at the beginning of March, 2020, I had not yet joined the 10-day intermittent fasting challenge with Dr. Ellen Britt, PA, Ed.D. and Denise Wakeman. I don't believe I even mentioned this Challenge to him on that day, as I was preparing to host my live event in Los Angeles over the following week and was preoccupied with getting everything in order.

Ready to Make Serious Changes to My Health... I Surrender

At 302 pounds and sixty-four years of age, I was now ready to surrender to the idea that I needed ongoing help to get to and maintain a healthy weight for the remainder of my life. And I intended this "remainder" to be long, fruitful, and filled with joyous activity. How I was going to accomplish this feat was still just out of my grasp, but I was beginning to imagine a life of possibilities and hope.

I would be a part of the Medicare system within a few months, and relegated to the status of senior citizen with all the benefits, myths, and assumptions that designation entails.

Finally, I could admit out loud that I alone was powerless in this struggle, and that doing more of the same would only lead to same results I had already experienced.

CHAPTER 5

Health and Wellness Go Together

"The real secret to lifelong good health is actually the opposite: Let your body take care of you."

~ Deepak Chopra

A holistic approach to overall health and wellness allows us each to adopt the habits and goals that we desire, all while eliminating the wrong foods in favor of more nutritional ones, seeking an activity level based on our needs and individual abilities, and engaging in self-care regimes that will serve us well. The whole personage is embraced and supported.

I'll use the alternate spelling – wholistic – to describe the four-pronged approach I've taken with my own intermittent fasting practice, as well as with the two people I am coaching in this area since becoming a Certified Intermittent Fasting Coach. The word wholistic relates to the philosophy that all parts of a thing – in this case a human – are interconnected.

Think of your life as being physical, emotional, intellectual, and psychological/social. The physical part includes what you see in your reflection in the mirror, as well as what others see. This can all be broken down statistically to represent the numbers that make you who you are, like height, weight, blood pressure, and so on.

Your thoughts and feelings constitute your emotional guidance system that dictates how you perceive your circumstances and the world around you.

The intellectual part of you consists of your mind, and how it guides your thoughts, beliefs, and actions.

The psychological you is where we live most of the time. When it comes to your health, you may have an accurate read on where you are right now. Or, you may have an inaccurate, distorted thought process around this area of your life.

For example, earlier I shared that I always felt like an outsider around people my age while growing up. Always is an absolute that is seldom accurate.

As I'm writing this, I'm thinking back to the summer of 1966 when I had more friends than I could count. My weight didn't seem like an issue. A cute boy named Billy told me he liked me and I graciously turned down his offer to go steady.

It was a fun-filled summer vacation that paved the way for me to have more friends, experiences, and joy than ever before. Obviously, thinking about my life in absolutes is just a figment of my imagination.

Turning 65 during the summer of 2020 was the final wakeup call I needed to address my issues with food and weight, and this quest became one to not only change my eating habits and drop a significant amount of weight, but also one to reinvent my life in a way that would give me almost total control over my destiny.

By then, there were some absolutes. My A1C was dangerously close to my becoming an insulin dependent diabetic for the remainder of my life.

In fact, as I've mentioned previously Dr. El Tom had already begun ordering several medications and diabetic supplies for me, but I remained in denial of this dire situation. If I didn't acknowledge my situation, I could pretend it didn't exist.

Intermittent fasting literally saved my life, as the COVID-19 virus started the pandemic. It was quickly discovered that people who were morbidly obese, diabetic, living with underlying health conditions, and over the age of sixty were the most likely to be hospitalized if they contracted the virus. They were also more likely to be severely ill, placed on a ventilator, and not surviving the ordeal.

By changing the hours I would consume food each day, along with eating food that was more wholesome, I significantly improved my chances to stay alive. I honestly saw it this way and continue to believe this as fact.

I am not dramatic by nature, but you must admit that the idea of being able to save your own life, simply by making a few simple and doable changes to your lifestyle is an emotion driven concept. And I felt very fortunate to have begun my intermittent fasting practice at the exact time the world went on lockdown.

Health Issues Brought About by Obesity and Diabetes

Growing up and going into young adulthood, I did not know anyone personally who was diabetic. Actually, the truth is that we all know people who are dealing with diabetes every day, but most of the time they do not discuss it openly.

Fortunately for me, I was able to reverse the effects of my prediabetes in time to avoid many of the health issues that were sure to follow in the coming months and years.

One of these is something called diabetic retinopathy. I was not familiar with this until a woman in the Fast Factor group I'm in with Denise Wakeman and Dr. Ellen Britt, PA, Ed.D. shared her story with us.

She had been diagnosed with severe nonproliferative retinopathy the year before she began her intermittent fasting practice. At that time, the doctors were sure she would lose her vision, at least partially and no longer be able to drive and do other things in her life where full vision is necessary. She was in her fifties and had dreams of traveling, starting a business, and being involved in her young grandchildren's lives.

As you can imagine, she was gripped with fear by what the remainder of her life would be like if her vision dwindled away to the point where everything she wanted and needed to do each day would be affected. But she was open to making the necessary changes to her lifestyle and found IF to be an answer to her prayers.

As of this writing her vision has been almost fully restored to what she had twenty or more years earlier, and her future in bright and filled with achieving her dreams and goals.

Diabetic Retinopathy

People with both Type 1 and Type 2 diabetes are at a heightened risk for eye complications and peripheral neuropathy.

You may have heard that diabetes causes eye problems and may lead to blindness. People with diabetes do have a higher risk of blindness than people without diabetes.

There are four stages of diabetic retinopathy:
- Mild Nonproliferative is the beginning stage where swelling begins in the blood vessels of the retina. Leaking may begin to occur in this stage.
- Moderate Nonproliferative is where the blood vessels essential for nourishing the retina become blocked. Swelling and leaking are occurring in the blood vessels.
- Severe Nonproliferative is an advanced stage where the blood vessels are blocked and the retina is no longer receiving the blood supply it needs to function normally.
- Proliferative is the final, advanced stage of retinopathy. Signals have been sent to grow new blood vessels, and these grow in an abnormal state. Because of where they are grown along the retina, leaking of blood causes severe vision loss and may lead to blindness

Gum Disease

I had no idea that even being labeled as prediabetic put you at risk for gum disease. During the spring of 2020 I visited my dentist for routine x-rays and a cleaning. While the hygienist poked around my mouth with her tools, she got a look on her face that told me she shouldn't play poker.

Something was wrong and before I could ask her what she was

seeing she had summoned the dentist to lean in for a closer look.

He focused on my lower left quadrant and then asked,

"Have you felt this tooth getting loose?"

NO! I hadn't felt anything and wasn't aware of any changes in my oral health. I'd had a cleaning four months earlier and thought I was brushing and flossing adequately to maintain my dental health.

"Are you diabetic?" was his follow up question.

Before I could answer he held the x-rays in front of me so I could see what was happening.

My pockets had deepened significantly during the past year. The x-rays showed a level of periodontal disease that I would never have predicted, given my obsession with dental care and willingness to go for three times a year for cleanings and checkups.

Seemingly overnight, I had a loose molar – tooth #31 if you're familiar with the dental numbering system – and a few days later an oral surgeon extracted it. I keep the small plastic package containing the tooth in the top drawer in my bathroom. My high blood sugar levels over the previous couple of years led to my oral health decline. I never knew this was even a remote possibility and outcome and I am determined not to lose another tooth.

Diabetes causes blood vessel changes. The thickened blood vessels can reduce the flow of nutrients and removal of wastes from body tissues. This reduced blood flow can weaken the gums and bone. This puts them at greater risk for infection.

Diabetes that is not controlled well leads to higher blood sugar (glucose) levels in the mouth fluids. This promotes the growth of bacteria that can cause gum disease. On the other hand, infections from untreated periodontal disease can cause the blood sugar to rise and make it harder to control diabetes.

These diabetes-related factors, together with poor oral hygiene, can lead to periodontal disease. These are the most common symptoms of gum disease:

- Red, swollen, sore gums
- Receding gums
- Loose or separating teeth

- ◉ Bleeding while brushing or flossing
- ◉ Pus between the teeth and gums
- ◉ A change in bite and jaw alignment

The symptoms of gum disease may seem like other health conditions. See a dentist or other oral health specialist for a diagnosis.

It's very important to share your diabetes history with your dentist, especially how well your blood glucose is controlled. In addition to your health history, the dentist will:

- ◉ Check your gums for any sign of inflammation
- ◉ Take X-rays to find out if there is bone loss
- ◉ Measure any pockets around your teeth

If you have gum disease, the dentist may refer you to a periodontist. These are dentists who are experts in the diagnosis and treatment of gum disease. A periodontist will evaluate your teeth and gums and give you treatment options for your condition.

But better yet, use intermittent fasting to lose some weight and lower your blood sugar so you can take control of gum disease and other health issues.

CHAPTER 6

Anti-Aging and Autophagy

"Age is just a number. Life and aging are the greatest gifts that we could possibly ever have."

~ Cicely Tyson

I like to tell people that when it comes to intermittent fasting, I initially came aboard for the weight loss but I've stayed for the anti-aging and other health benefits.

There's something called autophagy that I was first introduced to in March of 2020, soon after beginning my IF practice. It's the body's way of cleaning out and sloughing off the old and damaged cells, in order to regenerate newer, healthier cells, according to Priya Khorana, PhD, in Nutritional Education from Columbia University. "Auto" means self and "phagy" means eat, so the literal meaning of autophagy is "self-eating."

I've begun reading medical journals and was thrilled to discover that anyone may have a complimentary subscription to resources such as the New England Journal of Medicine. According to an article they published in the June 24th, 2021 issue, autophagy serves to protect the cell from cytotoxicity through degradation of toxic protein aggregates, pathogens, and damaged organelles. It also sustains homeostasis by recycling essential metabolites.1 Autophagy involves the formation of a transient double membrane–bound autophagosome that encapsulates and delivers cytoplasmic cargo to acidic sub compartments of the endolysosomal system for degradation by hydrolysis.

I don't know about you, but most of this previous paragraph went over my head. This is what Dr. David Jockers, DNM, DC says about autophagy and cellular healing:

"Autophagy is your body's natural method of detoxification. It happens when your body recycles and gets rid of old and unhealthy cells allowing the creation of new and healthy cells to replace them. While fasting, fasted exercise, and eating a ketogenic diet are three of the most powerful ways to enhance autophagy, we can't forget about the importance of anti-inflammatory herbs and compounds to enhance autophagy and improve your health."

This information is included in his book, *The Fasting Transformation: A Functional Guide to Burn Fat, Heal Your Body and Transform Your Life with Intermittent and Extended Fasting that was published* in May of 2021.

Dr. Jockers continues by saying that "Autophagy is an essential part of your immune system. It is a process that happens when your body recycles and expels old or excess cells that don't benefit or potentially harm your health. It is also referred to as a process of self-eating. Autophagy happens as a result of cellular stressors, such as nutrient deprivation from fasting, exercise, or significant temperature change.

So how does cellular stress drive autophagy? Your body is constantly striving for homeostasis or physiological balance for survival. Stress, on the other hand, refers to an environment that demands change.

As a result, autophagy helps your body to function better. With the help of new mitochondria and healthy cells, your body becomes stronger. It also becomes more resilient to chronic stress, inflammation, chronic pain, and disease."

Autophagy is your body's natural method of achieving detoxification. This occurs when your body is able to recycle and eliminate old and unhealthy cells to allow the creation of new and healthy cells to replace them. While you are fasting, getting exercise, and eating a more healthy and natural diet are three of the most powerful ways to enhance your own autophagy. And don't forget about the importance of anti-inflammatory herbs and compounds to enhance autophagy and improve your health.

The Deeper Benefits of Autophagy

As if the mere sloughing off and eliminating tired and worn-out cells was not enough, there are also a number of additional benefits we can't overlook. In fact, finding out this information early on made me a fan of autophagy before I even reached that level in my own body. These include:

⦿ Getting rid of old cells

Senescent cells are older cells that don't function at a high level anymore. While it is normal for your cells to age, it is also important to replace these senescent cells with new ones. Autophagy helps to remove old cells with new and healthy cells.

⦿ Improving mitochondrial health

The mitochondria are the powerhouse of your cell that is essential for energy production and overall health. Unless regular bouts of autophagy are stimulated, you end up with dysfunctional and metabolically inflexible mitochondria. Autophagy may help to degrade dysfunctional mitochondria and replace it with new ones.

⦿ Eliminating viral infected cells

As opposed to bacteria, yeast, and parasites, viruses are intracellular pathogens that impact your cellular genetic. A strong immune system can put viruses into a dormant state; however, it doesn't actually get rid of them. Autophagy is your body's natural way of removing infected cells and replacing them with healthy ones.

⦿ Reducing apoptosis
Older cells undergo programmed cell death called apoptosis. However, this process is very stressful on your body and may lead to inflammation. Autophagy, on the other hand, is a much more energy-efficient process that helps to get rid of old cells and create new ones.

⦿ Creating a stronger, more stress resilient body and mind
Autophagy helps your cells to become stronger and healthier, and your body to become more resilient to stress. It may help to reduce inflammation, including gut inflammation and the risk of leaky gut syndrome, and may help your brain health, mood, memory, and mental processing.

My Personal Benefits from Autophagy

I like to write down the details of what occurs each time I uncover a new benefit of intermittent fasting to my life experience. Here, I'll share some of them with you in the hope that by simply reading these, at least one of them will resonate with you.

I had already been taking a collagen powder supplement for two years before I started my IF practice, based on my ongoing issues with my Achilles tendon. This situation followed a fall in the fall of 2018 that left me with a broken kneecap.

Collagen is known to be helpful for joint and tendon problems. But within three months of beginning IF, my skin, hair, and nails began to noticeably change. My skin is so soft I find myself caressing my arms and legs as I sit at my desk writing each day. My hair is shinier and my nails are stronger.

Also, the ringing in my ears, commonly known as tinnitus, that I had begun to think of as being permanent, slowly came to a complete stop. Up to twenty percent of the population experiences this high-pitched ringing sound that is completely internal and not heard by others around you. It's most typical among people over the age of fifty and may be accompanied by some degree of dizziness or lightheadedness.

It is worth it to me to shorten my feasting window on most days to make sure autophagy kicks in regularly. This is an ongoing area of science that is making a difference to millions of people around the world. Who know what others benefits I am experiencing with my health that are on the inside of my body?

Being able to wear hats again! I mentioned earlier that I had become a "fat head" and was keenly aware that while most people had a normal and proportionate size head, mine appeared to be what I referred to as "freakishly" large. This phenomenon was due to the massive amount of subcutaneous fat that had built up on my scalp. I don't remember exactly when it occurred or how much weight I had lost, but one day on a Zoom webinar I noticed that my head was now a normal size and my glasses fit my face more comfortably.

Sitting cross-legged in bed to read, watch a favorite movie or listen to music was something I thought I would never experience again. But one day, I tried it more out of curiosity than for any other reason, and it worked!

Ketosis: Is Intermittent Fasting Superior to a Ketogenic Diet?

Again, I will mention Dr. Ellen Britt, PA, Ed.D. and Denise Wakeman, the two women who helped me get started with IF back in March of 2020, and to whom I stay in close contact with through our Fast Factor Circle to continue to improve my overall health. They run an active membership group that I've been a part of since I began my IF journey.

They have a publication called The IF Insider and you may subscribe to it at https://ifinsider.substack.com/. They describe this as *"your briefing on the most compelling developments in intermittent fasting."* This subject has become so controversial over the years and it's important to have access to the most up to date information and research so you will be able to make decisions for yourself based on experience and science.

"What is the difference between ketosis caused by intermittent

fasting and a ketogenic diet?"

This question was asked by one of the participants in our current 10-Day Fast Factor Intermittent Fasting Challenge. Because many of our participants are relatively new to fasting, there is naturally some confusion around the topic of ketosis. But even experienced intermittent fasters may have questions, so we thought we would address this topic here.

Let's define ketosis. But first, a lesson in basic nutrition is in order to help you understand things more easily.

All foods can be grouped into one of three categories, called macronutrients or "macros" for short: protein, carbohydrates or "carbs" and fats. Your body breaks down and uses carbohydrates and fats for energy and uses the components in protein as the building blocks for the biological machinery of the body to make enzymes, hormones, and muscle, among other things.

Carbohydrates are broken down into sugars, primarily glucose which is used to fuel your cells. A short-term supply is stored in your liver in the form of glycogen, to get you through short periods when you can't eat. Any excess glucose is stored as fat.

As you fast daily, the glycogen stores in your liver are gradually depleted and your body naturally turns to fat stores (around your abdomen and other areas) and begins to burn that fat for energy.

When you are eating a ketogenic diet, you are choosing to severely limit the amount of carbohydrates in your diet, as this "keto" diet as it's called, is nearly 75% fat. This diet forces your body to burn fat for fuel, as there are just not enough carbs available for the body's energy requirements.

Either way, by adopting the "keto" diet or by doing intermittent fasting, your body is at times using fat for fuel. Fats are broken down into triglycerides for use as energy but there are some cells in the body, namely your brain cells, which cannot use this form of fat directly. The fat is processed in the liver, and a by-product of that processing is something called ketone bodies which are used by the brain as fuel instead of the usual glucose that it normally burns.

Research has shown that ketones are a more efficient fuel than glucose, providing more energy per unit of oxygen used than sugar.

So why do intermittent fasting when you could just eat a keto diet all the time?

A keto diet, high in fat and very low in carbs, like all restrictive dietary programs, is simply not sustainable. People who are on keto diets may be more susceptible to kidney stones, as well as micronutrient deficiencies.

But in my opinion, here's one of the major differences: people who do daily intermittent fasting and have done it long enough to become fat-adapted, enjoy what is known as metabolic flexibility. This is the ability to easily burn carbs while eating and then easily switching to fat burning while fasting.

People who are depending on a keto diet to force their bodies into burning fat for fuel do not have this metabolic flexibility. Intermittent fasting is a much more natural, sustainable, and healthier way to achieve ketosis than forcing yourself to always be on a keto diet. So, keep calm and fast on!

SECTION 3

WHAT IF YOU BEGIN TO FAST INTERMITTENTLY?

"The starting point of all achievement is desire."

~ Napoleon Hill

Making the decision to begin an intermittent fasting practice is a personal one. For me, it made sense on many levels. Like Napoleon Hill wrote decades ago, the starting point of all achievement is desire. I had a strong desire to live a life that was unencumbered by excess weight, diminished wellness, and premature aging.

I desperately needed to drop a significant amount of weight to get my health back on the right track. My A1C, the measure of blood sugar levels in the body over the previous three months, was creeping higher with every visit to my doctor. Dr. El Tom had told me that if I lost even ten percent of my weight - at that time it was about thirty pounds - I would begin to move closer to the normal readings for this.

The A1C blood test is the primary tool used to diagnose diabetes and pre-diabetes and to monitor blood glucose control in people with type 1 and type 2 diabetes. This test enables health care providers to diagnose diabetes and treat it before more serious complications occur and to diagnose pre-diabetes to prevent or delay the development of type 2 diabetes.

There is much discussion and disagreement about the exact numbers and what they represent, but suffice it to say that a reading of less than about 5.7 is considered to be in the normal range, between 5.7 and 6.4 is in the pre-diabetic range, and anything 6.5 or higher represents full onset diabetes. Be sure to consult with your physician to discuss where you are right now with your A1c.

Diabetes is an epidemic in many countries in the world, and in all of North America. There are so many complications that will most likely arise once you become diabetic, including major issues with your vision, circulation, and dental and gum health.

Secondly, I wanted my energy and stamina back. I was tired of being too exhausted to do the things I loved. I would be winded after walking up the stairs or around the mall. Just bending over to pick something up was uncomfortable and forced me to catch my breath. And having to shift sideways on the sofa to be able to put on shoes and socks was a daily reminder of how my body was suffering every day.

Finally, I wanted a chance to live my life as a healthy person once again. International and domestic travel, for both business and pleasure added a special something to my life. My business was successful. I was positive that I could use my "crossover" skills to be successful with my health as well.

Intermittent fasting was the answer to my prayers and to years of searching for the most simple and direct way to lose weight, keep it off, regain my health, and to feel youthful once again.

I came to believe in the concept of eating only for a specific number of hours each day, instead of grazing from sunrise to the time I went to bed. I believed in Dr. Ellen Britt, PA, Ed.D. and Denise Wakeman. I just needed to believe in myself enough to get started and see some initial results with an intermittent fasting practice.

My challenge to you is to keep an open mind, be willing to move ever so slightly out of your comfort zone, and become an expert when it comes to your body and mind. Question everything, do your research, then find the people you will trust to be on your team and a part of your village.

CHAPTER 7

A New Way of Eating/Living/Being

"Give a man health and a course to steer, and he'll never stop to
trouble about whether he's happy or not."

~ George Bernard Shaw

Intermittent fasting is not rocket science. It is a new way of life that suits my goals precisely, in terms of simplicity and ease, as well as my lifestyle. This practice does not promise overnight results. The people who are evangelists for this way of eating and living come from diverse backgrounds and circumstances. There appear to be as many people who choose IF for weight loss as those who come to it for reasons entirely based upon improving their health.

My initial goal was to lose weight; I soon realized that getting to my goal weight would be easier than I could ever have imagined. I've stayed for purely health reasons like autophagy, something I addressed in more specific and greater detail in the previous chapter.

Non-Scale Victories

The first victory I experienced that could not be measured was when I tried on a shirt I wanted to wear. It was a good friend's birthday and a few of us were going to gather in her backyard for a light lunch and birthday cake. I pulled the shirt over my head without thinking and was pleasantly surprised when it fit me so well.

This was my introduction to what we refer as "non-scale victories" or NSVs.

Denise Wakeman defines a "non-scale victory" as something positive that you can tell is happening as a result of your IF practice OTHER than weight loss. For most people, NSVs come before weight loss and they are important signs that you are on the right track. Some examples include...

- ⊙ increased energy
- ⊙ just plain feeling better
- ⊙ improved sleep
- ⊙ clothes fitting better
- ⊙ decrease in inflammation
- ⊙ an increased sense of confidence
- ⊙ surprise at discovering that fasting for "X" number of hours is possible for you

It wasn't long before each of these NSVs, and more arrived on my doorstep more regularly and I cheered each one and shared it with the group Dr. Ellen and Denise had set up for us.

There was the time when I had to move my car's seat up closer to the steering wheel; the time I put on my Fitbit and needed to move it up one notch to match my new, slender wrist; and the day I was able to slide in beside my grandson at a booth in our favorite restaurant.

These may seem like small things to you, or perhaps you can understand what I'm sharing here with you on a more personal level.

This might be my personal favorite in this regard... My ankles have returned and I no longer have "Fred Flintstone" feet!

Here is an article I published on the topic of non-scale victories...

Non-Scale Victories at the Top of the Escalator

Non-Scale Victories Come in Various Shapes and Sizes

In the spring of 2019, I put myself on a shopping hiatus. I had full closets in both of the cities I call home. Most of the clothing and even some of the shoes no longer fit me, but even without those items I had enough to last for several years or longer. My history with having issues around clothes and shoes is a long and winding one and goes back a few decades to a different time in my life.

I grew up insecure. Food insecure was the biggest one, long before this had a label. Clothing insecure also described my mother and I during a time when designer clothes were not a thing but fitting in with others was huge. My mother described me as being "hard on shoes" and I never understood the concept of being careful to protect and extend the life of one's clothing and shoes. I was a tomboy and could not separate out my feelings between being myself and making sure not to place too much wear and tear on my items.

There was one time when I had grown out of my shoes and got them terribly dirty simultaneously, at a time when we had little money for food and necessities and none set aside for new shoes. I was in the third grade and was all ready to go to school one morning when my mother looked down at my feet and frowned her disapproval. With no time or money at her disposal, she came up with the idea of cutting the fake fur off my bedroom slippers so we could begin our walk to my school. These days kids and adults alike have somewhat more freedom to be themselves and wear almost anything, but in those days it simply wasn't done. I can still hear the taunts of my classmates when I arrived at my classroom a few minutes after the morning bell had rung.

After I got home, I cried and blamed my mother for what had happened. She apologized, when she was not at fault and reminded me of the importance of taking care of my shoes so I would always have a pair to wear. She glossed over the problem of feet growing bigger and I wished for a new life for us both where food and clothes and everything else was in plentiful supply. And a dog; I also wished for a dog that day and named it Lassie, no matter what the breed would be.

Fast forward to my future as a young adult, where money flowed more easily and materials items were not often in short supply. The only thing left over from my childhood was the insecurity. Now I was insecure about my worth as a human and around forming and maintaining relationships of all kinds. A trip to the mall after payday meant a new outfit, shoes, and a purse or wallet. Then out to dinner somewhere special completed the evening. Sometimes I invited a friend to share the entire experience and paid for their clothes and meal as well. It felt good to be able to do this on occasion, but the feeling did not last. It was difficult for me to discern whether the person was a true friend or just someone along for the ride.

Decades pass by quickly, like a hummingbird swooping in for a drink out of the backyard feeder and then gone again in a blur. I'm a classroom teacher now and work in real estate pert-time. Money is tight at times. There's enough for a house and car payment, and a two-week vacation on an airplane every other summer. I subsidize my now elderly mother's Social Security check each month and also take her shopping for clothes and shoes after I get paid each month. We don't discuss the past. Too many sore spots around topics from my childhood. I dismiss them as not being important enough to rehash in the present. We both pretend to forget what was so painful in those moments.

In my forties I begin to put on weight. It wasn't noticeable at first. Then the pants were tight and at some point, I hung my belts on a hook in my closet and began wearing pants and skirts with stretchy waistbands. No more jeans, either, until some company came out with "pajama jeans" a client showed off at a conference we both attended. I smiled in agreement with her choice, but inside I was shocked at how horrible they looked on her.

When my business began to grow and I started speaking at live events, I had to find clothes that would not only fit me well, but also look professional. They also had to be comfortable. I asked a close friend to take me shopping where she was buying clothes and we ended up at a boutique style shop where she had me try on a number of outfits. It was in those moments I realized how little skill I had when it came to buying clothes that would serve me. The following month I went to the Macy's store at my local mall, determined to replicate the experience I'd had with my friend, closer to home and more frugally to fit my budget.

The "Women's" department was on the first floor, almost hidden between men's shoes and men's active wear. In fact, this was the only department for women on this floor, as almost the entire upper level was for women. But they carried no sizes larger than XL, which is "extra-large" for women. There were "Plus" sizes up to 3X, and fortunately for me I did not grow any larger than that over the years. No longer willing to torture myself by walking through an entire floor with nothing that would fit me, I began parking in the underground parking lot that had an entrance on the first floor.

Over the years I got to know the women who worked in this department, as well as some women who shopped there. We would often remark that the most people sales people tended to be assigned to this area. They would smile sweetly and patiently as the large women lamented over the fact that most of the clothes were *prints with huge flowers, childlike images, or vertical stripes. There were some more appealing colors and patterns, but they were few and far between.*

Once in a great while, I would leave this department and ride the escalator up to the second level. Usually this was so I could exit the store and end up in what was called the "Patio Shops" or to meet a friend or colleague at one of the restaurants or coffee shops. The Apple Store was also in the patio area and many a time I forgot my worries by looking at what was new and innovative in phones and computers to pass some time away.

Two non-scale victories today. The first was this morning when I put on my Fitbit after showering. It had become too loose and this time it fit perfectly in the next hole over on the band! The second one was when I went to Macy's for the first time in a year. I confidently rode the escalator to the second floor where almost all of the women's clothing is displayed. I did not buy anything, but I did spend ninety minutes looking through every rack on the entire floor. I can now find clothes that will fit me that are stylish and appealing. I even looked at bathing suits! Before today and for over a decade I had to shop in the Women's Plus Size section on the first floor, next to men's shoes and outerwear. I felt excluded from the mainstream and embarrassed when I saw someone I knew. Today is a day I will remember forever.

What does NSV mean?

If you've seen the abbreviation "NSV" on Instagram or Connect, or heard a Weight Watchers member use the term in a Workshop, you've probably wondered what it meant. The letters stand for "non-scale victories," the small, everyday indicators that mark your new, healthier life. Sounds like fun, right? Like an added bonus to the pounds dropping away?

But try thinking of it this way: The NSVs are what your hard work is really about. And as for the numbers on the scale? They're the added bonus. Sure, keeping track of the weight lost is an important part of the program. But also acknowledging your progress in other areas can help keep you positive.

For example, here are some non-scale victories that are well worth celebrating:

Your clothes fit better.

It's easier to walk up the stairs and play with your kids.

You have more energy.

You can put on your shoes more easily.

Your watch is hanging loosely on your wrist and you have to tighten it a notch.

You feel more positive and better about yourself.

You're noticing that you choose to eat more vegetables and drink more water. You're acting like a healthy person!

Non-scale victories have been few and far between during my lifetime. Now they're coming faster and more furiously than I ever could have imagined.

While I never thought of myself as being excluded from any groups or activities, looking back makes me realize that this did occur throughout the past couple of decades. People don't necessarily intend to be mean or unkind, I believe. But sometimes it's just easier not to have to deal with a person of size. That's how I began thinking of myself at some point in time. There are people of color and people of circumstance, so it makes sense that large people would be thought of as people of size.

As I stepped off the escalator recently, I was careful not to put too much weight on my left foot. I was wearing old shoes that were now coming apart! All I needed was to suffer a mishap with so many people around. And that's when the childhood memories came flooding back. I was in the 3rd grade again, wearing my bedroom slippers to school because I had no other choice of shoes to wear because we were poor.

But now I did have a choice. I promised myself I would throw away this pair of shoes when I got home, and to go through the dozens of pairs I had to see what could be given away and which pairs were still new in the box, being saved for a special occasion and not seeing the light of day. I have committed to making every day special, and to know that I am worth it in every sense of what that means. Now this is a non-scale victory of epic proportions!

Food, Weight, and Control

Food and eating represent a level of control in our lives. I wrote about this in an earlier chapter and wanted to follow up with this concept here. Whereas using food for control can be a negative experience, here we will turn it around to show the positive side.

I now know that I can control my weight, my body image, and my health with food. Wow, that's a powerful thought and belief as I am writing it here!

But throughout my life, I used food to limit my engagement with the outside world. Being overweight, especially more than a hundred pounds over the normal range for your height and build, gives you an excuse to exclude yourself from all kinds of activities and experiences.

My weight gave me permission to miss out on social engagement, to avoid romantic entanglements, to talk myself out of jobs and career opportunities, to step back from daring adventures, and to basically remain on the sidelines of my life experience.

Instead, I became a voyeur of sorts where I was existing in a parallel universe, looking in from the outside and playing at the most minimal level possible and always on the sidelines. I kept on telling myself that everything would change someday, knowing down deep that "someday" would never arrive.

This is a deeply psychological phenomena, from my personal experience. If I was the biggest person at the party, no one would ask me to dance or even smile at me in that special way that is a normal part of attraction. I could cheer for the players, without having to play.

I lived vicariously through other people's experiences for decades at a time, to the point that if felt normal and acceptable to me.

When I had lost about fifty pounds with intermittent fasting in the fall of 2020, I attended an evening fundraiser for my Rotary Club in person. Many of the people there did not recognize me. Both men and women alike, individually and within the group, told me how good I looked. I must have been beaming from ear to ear at their compliments, because when I woke up the next morning my face was a bit sore from all of the smiling I had done.

But I have zero regrets for being all smiles that night at the fundraiser. Instead, I am focused on the future and feeling stronger, more positive, and happy than ever before.

What If You're Not Losing Weight with Intermittent Fasting?

To answer this question, I went directly to Dr. Ellen. The following appeared on the IF Insider, a publication written by Ellen Britt, PA, Ed.D. She and Denise Wakeman distribute it regularly on Substack as the IF Insider.

Why Aren't I Losing Weight?

One of the most frequently asked questions we get from people who are early into their intermittent fasting practices (usually from a couple of weeks to a couple of months) goes something like this:

"Maybe intermittent fasting is not for me! I've been fasting daily now for X weeks and I haven't lost a single pound. I am ready to throw in the towel. Help!"

When we hear this question, the first thing we do is gather more information in the form of four crucial questions:

One - Are you clean fasting?

The first thing to determine is that your fast is clean, meaning that during your fasting time, you are not eating anything and are drinking ONLY plain water, sparkling water unflavored or unsweetened either naturally or artificially, plain green or black tea unflavored or unsweetened either naturally or artificially, or black coffee (caffeinated or decaf) unflavored or unsweetened either naturally or artificially.

Most people find it strange that we say not to drink anything flavored and/or sweetened even artificially, as those beverages would have zero calories. Here's the thing: there is evidence that flavors (natural or artificial), as well as zero-calorie sweeteners, have the ability to "trick" the body into thinking that food is on the way. In response, your body starts to put out insulin which is a signal for your body to store fat. Exactly what you don't want! So, the first thing is to make sure you are fasting clean.

Two - Are you overeating in your feasting window? (too many or the wrong kinds of calories)

Even though IF is NOT a diet, and we don't routinely count calories, it is possible to overeat during your feasting window. If you have, for example, an 8-hour feasting window as you would have in a 16:8 schedule, make sure you are not grazing the entire time. You'll likely just want to do maybe one larger meal, a smaller meal and maybe a snack and not eat at all in between. Eat only until you are satisfied and not stuffed. Having said that, this takes some getting used to and you will overeat or undereat early on until your body adjusts. You could also choose to track your calories for a few days with an app like Lose It! so you can more accurately gauge your average calorie intake.

Make sure you are eating as healthy as possible, with minimal refined and processed carbs. Whole grains, fresh fruits, lean meats (if you eat meat), and plenty of fresh vegetables should do the trick.

Three - Are you undereating in your feasting window? (not enough calories)

It's also possible you could be under eating in your feasting window. This is especially true if you have just started and are only a week or two in. You will gradually adjust and will be able to eat more as time goes by. You may want to use an app like Lose It! to track your calories for a few days to make sure you are eating enough.

When you chronically undereat (as most "diets" have you do) your metabolism will naturally slow down as your body thinks you are starving and is trying to protect you by holding on to your stores of body fat. You have to eat enough so that does not happen. Usually, following the rule of thumb to eat only until satisfied, not stuffed works well.

Four - How many hours a day are you fasting? (What is the length of your fasting window?)

If you are good to go with the first three questions, the last thing to do is to look at the length of your fasting window. Most people start out their IF practices with a 16:8 window, sixteen hours of fasting, and an eight-hour eating window. For some folks that works just fine as a permanent schedule, but for many people who want to lose weight, it's just not enough to do the trick.

Try lengthening your fasting window by a half hour or one hour increment and see how this works for the next several weeks. If this does not do the trick, you may need more help.

Why It Matters - It's really important to be able to troubleshoot your progress with IF, especially if you are doing it to lose weight. Using the four questions model can help you do that.

If You Need to Lose 50 Pounds or More

Recently, I was at an event for one of the non-profits I'm involved with in my community. There were people in attendance who had not seen me in person since before I began my IF practice in March of 2020 and they did not recognize me over a year later. I've come to love this experience, as it gives me an opportunity to talk about my experience in a poignant and dramatic manner.

On this day, we were inside having lunch before going back outside for the fundraising portion of the event. I found myself standing in front of a semi-circle of people who began asking me questions. It was as though I were a speaker at a live event, something I've been doing regularly since 2008.

I quickly made eye contact with each person and realized there were at least two groups of people standing before me. The first group was predominantly made up of women, aged fifty and older and who needed to lose at least fifty pounds. The remainder of the people were both men and women who were either at a healthy weight already or who could stand to lose twenty pounds or so.

Now, of course I could not determine who among these people

had one or more health issues and conditions for which intermittent fasting would be helpful, and I am not a doctor or other medical professional. But I went ahead and made the assumption that everyone there on that day would be interested in some way when I began to share my story.

I began by saying that I had been able to successfully drop over a hundred pounds using intermittent fasting, and that I was very close to achieving my goal weight.

Then, I added that I had been diagnosed as being prediabetic in the months leading up to my decision to go on this journey. I also shared that I was a four-time cancer survivor and that everything I was doing was with the approval and under the supervision of my personal physician.

I could see in their eyes and their body language that they were riveted with hearing my story. One lady asked if I ate every day, and that's when I pulled up a chair and told them to do the same.

Over the next fifteen minutes I answered each of their questions as thoroughly and concisely as possible. It was evident that some of the people were interested strictly with the weight loss aspect, while others were more concerned with the overall health benefits of starting an intermittent fasting practice.

You have the same questions, I'm sure, and my goal in writing this book is to share my own story, to dispel any myths, and to generate interest in further exploration of this topic.

In the Preface, I told you that I had lost a hundred pounds previously. It was during 2004, the year I turned forty-nine years old. I achieved this goal the old-fashioned way, meaning that I earned every pound lost by starving by body and exercising in an extreme way.

Every couple of weeks I would go off this "diet" I had created for myself and return to the way of eating I was used to throughout much of my lifetime. I'd stuff myself from the time I awoke, up until my head was about to hit the pillow with all of the foods my body had become accustomed to over my lifetime. Sweets of all kinds were my favorites, followed by simple carbohydrates, processed foods, and various forms of dairy products.

It was a dangerous way to eat and live. Losing weight during that time did more harm than good in the overall scheme of things.

My cholesterol, blood pressure, and A1C went to dangerous levels, I began to have heart palpitations, and two doctors told me I would probably put back all the weight I was losing, and more, by dieting in this way. It wasn't that I didn't believe them, but more that I didn't care what they were advising me to do. I told myself that at least I wasn't taking any diet pills or supplements that could permanently harm my health.

It was during this period that I seriously considered having gastric bypass surgery, as I also first mentioned here in this book in the Preface. This was a turning point in my life and I believe it bears repeating.

My primary physician gave me a referral to a gastroenterologist and I went for the initial consultation.

While I was in the waiting room, I spoke with three women who were there for follow up visits. By the time I went in to speak with the doctor, I had already decided not to go through with the surgery for a variety of reasons.

As I drove home that day, I can remember feeling very sad and alone. I honestly believed that staying on my low-calorie diet and exercising as much as possible was the best way for me to drop the hundred extra pounds I had been asking my body to support for me.

I did achieve that goal, and the weight began to creep back on beginning the following day. I felt helpless in my struggle to maintain a healthy weight and knew that this issue was my weakness in life. My goal then became to only allow myself to gain ten or twenty pounds and then starve myself until I lost some of it again.

This yo-yo dieting was reminiscent of my teenage years. I knew it was not a solution to a much deeper problem, that it was only a band-aid for something that needed to be addressed in a different way. But I felt powerless in this area of my life and allowed my weight to affect every other area in the process.

It wasn't until 2020, more than sixteen years later that I would discover intermittent fasting. This revelation came quite by chance, and only because I knew two people who were having great success with it and helping others to do the same. These people are ones I will mention and refer to throughout this book – Dr. Ellen Britt, PA, Ed.D. and Denise Wakeman, friends and colleagues who are helping me to change my life forever, in a healthy and permanent way. These women, along with my personal physician, Dr. Bassem El Tom are the people I turn to regularly to make sure what I am doing in my IF practice is serving me in a holistic way.

What, How, and When Will You Eat?

Most often I am asked what I eat when speaking with someone with whom I have been telling about the way I've reinvented myself with intermittent fasting.

They first assume that I go for days at a time without eating, which is a common belief. I even held this belief before I began my IF practice in March of 2020. Whereas this is one of the models of eating used by people, it isn't the most common or the most popular. I'll go over the different schedules for intermittent fasting here:

12:12 Chances are you've gone at least 12 hours between dinner one evening and breakfast the following morning many times. If so, you've practiced the most basic form of intermittent fasting known as the 12:12 overnight fast. This means that you are fasting for 12 hours and then opening your feasting window up for the 12 remaining hours. I recommend beginners start here, then work their way up the fasting ladder as comfort and schedule permit.

I was actually eating on more of a 10:14 schedule for many years, meaning that I would only go without food for about ten, or even fewer at times, hours and eat for at least 14 hours each day. My body never had time to rest and recover from the volumes of food I was consuming every day.

There are some metabolic benefits from 12:12, and also you are enhancing your circadian rhythm - the 24 hour "awake/asleep" cycle that controls the human genome. Consuming some food helps you wake up in the morning, and a lack of food, starting in the evening helps you to sleep through the night.

The 16:8 schedule of fasting, with an 8 hour "feasting" window is a favorite of the majority of people practicing intermittent fasting. During the time I kept this schedule, I started eating around 11am or noon and ended by no later than 7pm. Remember, you may eat during any hours of your choosing, and if you need flexibility to eat with others or for any other reason, simply shift your schedule earlier or later for that day or longer. The important thing is to listen to your body and practice what works best for you at all times.

18:6… I'm dyslexic and it was only due to my confusing my numbers that I went from a 16:8 to an 18:6 overnight. It was a few days before I realized my mistake and what had occurred as a result, and by then I was used to my new 6 hour "feasting" window and 18 hours of fasting.

OMAD – The *One Meal A Day* schedule, is fairly self-explanatory: You eat all your daily calories in one sitting. I've learned that in order to promote a healthy circadian rhythm and sleep schedule, it's best to eat this meal while the sun is shining.

Other Types of IF include ADF (Alternate Day Fasting), Extended Fasting 5:2 with 5 days of eating for 8 to 10 hours, followed by 2 days of total fasting. I've never done this, and the people guiding me do not recommend it either.

CHAPTER 8

Paying It Forward

"It is health that is real wealth, and not pieces of gold and silver."

~ Mahatma Gandhi

One of the greatest joys in life is serving others with the knowledge, experience, and resources I have accumulated over time. Until I took control of my health with intermittent fasting, this typically meant serving others in the areas of online marketing strategies, entrepreneurship, authorship, time management, productivity, and mindset.

I'm thrilled that people now come to me to learn more about losing weight and improving their health, specifically with issues they are dealing with, and in general.

Each time I speak with someone about taking control of their health and significantly improving their day-to-day life, I know that my words will make a difference in their life from that day forward.

Becoming a Certified IF Coach

During the fall of 2020, I completed a six-month course of study with Dr. Ellen Britt, PA, Ed.D. and Denise Wakeman. This led to me becoming a Certified Intermittent Fasting Coach and taking on my first client at the end of the year. I added another in the early spring of 2021 and believe that mentoring two people at a time is an excellent fit for my goals and schedule.

My first client is the daughter of very close friends. She has just turned 30 and is now well on her way to improved health and wellness.

Hannah had been overweight since she was a little girl. As she grew older, the weight became an obstacle to her goals and dreams.

My second client, Rob, is in his early fifties and runs a busy printing company on the East Coast of the U.S. He had a mild heart attack in the summer of 2020 and his adult children begged him to lose weight and change his lifestyle.

When Your Photos Speak a Thousand Words

I've been a role model to thousands of people over the years with the success I continue to experience as a writer, publisher, and entrepreneur. So, it did not surprise me one iota when I began inspiring people to lose weight and to embrace a healthier lifestyle through intermittent fasting.

Posting photos of me engaged in certain activities became fun, as I hadn't been inclined to do this in the past. Then one day I posted four photos of me as a montage to show how my body had changed over the previous couple of years.

Because this journey is such a personal one, I believe that the message I am conveying will land on people in the best possible way. Instead of bragging about my new svelte body and the healthy glow I enjoy, inside and out, I'm showing what's possible. The premise of the message shares my precept that "If I can do it, so can you!"

Children Struggling with Obesity

My most recent project is a six-week program I host in my community for children struggling with obesity. It's for boys and girls, but so far only one boy has shown up. They range in age from twelve to seventeen and this program is helping them.

I only wish I could have begun working with young people in this way when I was in the early stages of my intermittent fasting practice, so they could have witnessed my physical transformation firsthand.

But that coincided with the beginning of the pandemic, when none on us were meeting in person unless it was absolutely necessary.

But instead of having regrets, I'm moving forward and helping this demographic to figure out how they will navigate the waters of healthy eating when there are so many temptations and misinformation.

I find that younger people are much more open-minded when it comes to choosing a window of time each day in which to eat. They tend to choose a feasting window of eight hours a day (this is the 16:8 model) to begin with, and then practice with moving that window earlier or later to accommodate their schedule.

One high school age girl showed me the schedule she had written down for herself. It was the same Monday through Thursday, and then shifted to later in the day on Friday through Sunday. She explained to me that this works for her because of social commitments she has with friends and family, where food is the focus of their time together. I don't believe she is a natural "foodie"; she simply wants to be included in activities with people and is making intermittent fasting work for her schedule. I applauded her for her mindfulness and know she is a role model to those she comes in contact with each day.

Being a Role Model to Family, Friends, and Community

Since changing my life from the inside out, beginning with leaving my job as a classroom teacher and working in real estate on a part-time basis to become an online entrepreneur in 2006, I have thought of myself as something of a role model to others.

This is an article I wrote after reverting to my previous eating habits and suffering the consequences. It was an important juncture in my journey and one that reminded me of how far I've come.

My Walk on the Wild Side

It was the final week of a year that almost broke many people around the world. I was one of the lucky ones in 2020, or so it felt to me. My health was good. My business was growing. My family was happy. But something was still missing in my life.

Three days before Christmas I had a call with Hannah, the young woman with whom I would begin working with in January of 2021. She is the adult daughter of my close friends. I've known her for more than five years but we had never had a serious conversation. She was nice enough, and pleasant but there was something that had kept her from getting too close to me all this time.

I knew what it was, this unspoken thing forming a wall between us. I could feel her looking at me when I was in the den with her parents and she was coming in or leaving the house. A quick "hello" without making eye contact and then she was gone. I had attempted to engage her in conversation on a number of occasions. The last time was two years ago at the park when the non-profit I volunteer with had a picnic. Before I could say hello, she slipped away and I didn't see her again that afternoon.

Hannah didn't want to be around me because I reminded her of herself in twenty-five years or so — overweight and alone. When I got home from the picnic I undressed and stood in front of my full-length mirror. How did I get to where I was? I was thinking this out loud and sat down on the cool tile floor and cried.

That was in the fall of 2019. I was now committed to losing weight and turning my health around. I would make it a goal for 2020. Not a resolution, mind you. A goal. A goal to be well thought out, pondered, and set in place. A goal that was different than a dream. A dream without a plan is simply a wish. My goal to lose one hundred pounds during 2020 would be a goal with a plan. My dream could be realized. After spending a full week in planning for the new year, setting goals, reviewing previous goals and achievements, and finally getting it all just the way I wanted it, I closed my legal-size planner and went to bed.

January came and went in a flash. My business was doing very well. I was publishing yet another book. Everything seemed to be falling into place, but one thing was still gnawing away at me. February arrived with a welcome rainstorm and unwanted heavy winds. Each day I went through my morning routine. I wrote, showered, volunteered, wrote some more, spent time with friends, and went to bed by nine. Each day I reviewed my goals and course corrected anything that needed to be revised. I went through the motions of living a full life, when it was anything but. Each day I was avoiding the one thing that mattered most to me. All this time and I still had no plan to lose five pounds, let alone a hundred. I couldn't look myself in the mirror because I was literally the elephant in the room.

February was coming to a close. A visit to the doctor showed that my weight was up to 302 and my A1C was on the high side of being "pre-diabetic." The doctor insisted on ordering several prescriptions, a glucose monitor, and other supplies. After the fourth text from the pharmacy, I finally drove over and picked it up.

"I'll pay for all of this stuff, but I'm not diabetic. I'm going to lose weight," I announced to the lady ringing up my order. She smiled without looking up from the register as I took the large white bag and walked with a purpose out to my car.

At the end of February, 2020, I received an email from Denise Wakeman about a 10 Day Challenge for people interested in losing weight and getting healthy. I've known Denise since first coming online as an entrepreneur in 2006. She was also going to be speaking at my marketing event in Los Angeles the first week of March. I signed up for the Challenge and knew I could ask her any questions about it while we were together. Also, it was scheduled to begin the day after my event ended. My thought was that I could still eat anything I wanted through that weekend, and then I would find out more about intermittent fasting. I mentally checked it off my list of goals to accomplish in 2020, even though I still didn't think of this as my plan to lose a hundred pounds.

Over that weekend the world shifted ever so slightly off its axis as the Coronavirus took hold. By Friday, March 13th the U.S. had called for a state of emergency. Flights were cancelled and store shelves emptied. I can remember visiting Sam's Club that weekend and being astounded at the sight of almost no meat or household essentials available. I was moving along every day with the Intermittent Fasting Challenge and seeing that this could actually work for me. By the end of the following week, I had become accustomed to eating for only an eight-hour window of time each day. Although I had yet to lose any weight, I was more comfortable in my skin and my focus each day was clearer than ever before in my memory. I signed up for the Fast Factor Circle run by Denise Wakeman and Dr. Ellen Britt, P.A, Ed.D. This would provide me with daily support and ongoing training as to how to make my fasting practice work for me on an ongoing basis.

Fast forward through the spring, past the summer, and into the fall of 2020 and I was on top of the world. Even with what was now called COVID-19 running rampant all over the planet, I was able to separate myself from this and focus on my life — my health and wellbeing, my family and other relationships, and my business. Oh, and I had begun losing weight by the very end of the Challenge and had now dropped a whopping 27% of my original body weight.

In November I began a Certification Program for Intermittent Fasting. Yes, I finally had a plan to achieve my weight loss goal and wanted to share my growing knowledge and ongoing experience with others in a professional coaching environment. Everyone who saw me even periodically over the previous seven or eight months remarked at how good I looked. I would beam and tell them that the doctors were thrilled that all of my numbers were now within the "normal" range and that I was having so much fun going shopping in my own closet!

Even though I would be completing my coaching certification program until the early spring of 2021, I was already thinking about working with my first client. And wouldn't you know it, I ran into my good friends at the Farmer's Market in Santa Barbara one Saturday morning and they wanted to know more about my dramatic weight loss and how young I looked. I briefly shared what I was learning about something called autophagy and how it was related to my intermittent fasting practice. Then they asked me if I could help their daughter, Hannah to have similar results.

Yes, Hannah is my first client. And when we spoke three days before Christmas in 2020, I was pleased to finally have the opportunity to connect with her. I took it slowly, knowing that her journey would be her own and that I was only there to guide her to a lifestyle that holds the promise of changing her life, forever. She wasn't very forthcoming on the phone.

I think it's more difficult to communicate with someone when you can't see their eyes and their smile. We exchanged holiday greetings and pleasantries. She began to apologize for not talking to me more when we saw each other, but I stopped her.

"Hannah, you're a young woman with your own life and friends. I did not expect you to abandon them and hang out with me."

There was a pause and then I continued.

"I saw those photos of you and your friends hiking up to Tupelo Ridge. The only way I would make it up that high is if a helicopter dropped me off at the top."

She laughed and I laughed a little louder. The ice was broken. Now we could talk.

I asked her if she was interested in trying intermittent fasting, or if it was just her mother's idea. A little of each, she told me. And then she started to tell me a story and the floodgates opened wide. No one can understand… All of my friends *are married... No one will ever love me... And it's the hardest at Christmas.*

The silence was deafening so I cleared my throat.

"You're right. I or anyone else can't understand. And I won't share my stories because they're boring and predictable. I take that back; I will share my stories with you as we get to know each other better. But not the boring ones, only the really exciting ones where I'm the superhero."

There was more laughter and that's when I asked her to tell me more about what she meant when she said it would be the hardest at Christmas.

Christmas Dinner - Intermittent Fasting

For the next half hour, she described in excruciating detail what the holidays were like with her family. Everyone was married, even the relative who lost his wife just after Christmas last year had recently remarried. Lots of kids, so many babies, and the women looking like models and fitting into their skinny jeans just months after a baby had arrived. And more food than anyone could imagine. Someone was always adding something new to the tables and for the four or five days everyone would be together it was almost non-stop eating. Someone would be watching her every moment to see what she was eating and how much. She said she felt like everyone was looking at her, but not truly seeing her. They felt sorry for her, she believed. But they also loathed spending time with a fat person.

"Some people act like they're allergic to fat, or that if they get too close to you, they'll catch it. They act like it's my fault."

I seized this opening.

"Why do you think you've been overweight for so long?"

"I don't exercise. I know I eat the wrong foods. I think my father was heavy, but I don't remember."

We discussed families and weight and fathers who were gone too soon. I was seeking commonality so that Hannah could trust me.

"You know our relationship around this is completely confidential. It has nothing to do with my friendship with your parents or with anyone else we mutually know. My hope is that we can share stories and ideas and recipes and successes with each other. Ones that other people won't care about or understand."

She liked that idea. Then we talked more about the week between Christmas Eve and New Year's Day and what it's like to be surrounded my people and food you love, and feeling like they are judging you every moment and won't love you if you eat too much.

"Connie, I know I'll be hiding food in my room and sneaking into the kitchen late at night to get more eggnog and dessert. I always hide food in my room when I'm staying with my family and I know that they know. And they won't mention it to me even if they see me shielding a plate of cookies from view on my way out of the kitchen. It's like this elephant in the room. And the thing that isn't funny at all is that I am that elephant."

I told her that the only thing I wanted her to focus on between now and when we would begin working together on January 4th was mindfulness. Enjoy the holidays, the people, the food, the gifts, and they joy of the season. But with everything you say or do or think about or eat, be mindful. I wanted her to get into the mindfulness habit to better face the situation and to be able to move on with my coaching after the first of the year.

We ended our call. I looked at the clock and saw that it was almost three in the afternoon. I quickly drove over to Trader Joe's and picked up a gallon of eggnog and some bakery items. I was about to enter a type of Twilight Zone – I was going to take a walk on the wild side.

Between the day before Christmas Eve and the day after New Year's Day – about eleven days – I allowed myself to slip back to my former habits. I was taking a break from my work online and had very few commitments related to my business. Because of the pandemic I would be staying at home throughout the month of December instead of traveling internationally to spend time with extended family in Europe. I carefully placed my items in the trunk of the car and drove home. I could already taste the eggnog!

What I experienced during this ten-day period was not what I had expected.

I thought I would give myself this time off as a break from my nine and a half month long intermittent fasting practice. I thought I would enjoy eating at all hours and anything I chose. I envisioned Hannah at her family's home, surrounded by people who loved her and wanted the best for her, yet continued to judge her on many levels. I thought of conversations I'd had with her parents, older sister, and a best friend from high school over the years.

Hannah had never had a boyfriend and didn't go to her High School Prom. She had friends but wasn't always invited to go places with them. Her sister's husband had told me they wanted to take her out in their boat but they thought it might be too awkward. At the time I had thought "too awkward for who, and how, exactly?" but I didn't say a word. I knew firsthand what it was like to be excluded at times because of your size and to pretend you didn't care when really you were hurting deep down inside.

My walk on the wild side reminded me of habits I had long since given up. One was eating candy right out the box or bag instead of a few pieces at a time. My home office began to fill up with everything I was bringing home. I would wake up in the morning and begin eating and drinking right away. My fasting practice consisted of an open window of "feasting" that lasted a few hours each day; what I was doing now was more like a free for all.

Then the achy joints set in, and the headaches, and the brain fog. And on the second or third day the ringing in my ears returned. I was bloated, tired, unhappy, and constipated. One day between Christmas and New Year's Eve I just couldn't force down another bite. As I set down the umpteenth glass of eggnog and another plate of cookies and a piece of pecan pie, I thought I'd finally had enough.

But the following morning I was ready for another eating marathon. If I were to properly serve Hannah and others like her — like me — then I needed to remember what it was like to be out of control with my eating. During the previous nine months I had dropped over eighty pounds. Now I had gained back three pounds and the pants that had fit so well just last week were now squeezing my stomach and thighs. I stopped going for my daily walks. I started staying up later at night and arising later each morning. My writing didn't come as easily. And could someone please make that ringing in my ears stop?!

On Saturday, the second day of January, 2021 I was ready to get back to my schedule. I gave away all the treats to the neighbors. I'd drank the last of the eggnog the night before and knew that the stores would not offer it again until next Christmas. I had learned much from my experiment. Now I wanted to connect with Hannah and see how her holidays had gone. I left a message on her phone and told her I was looking forward to officially working with her on Monday the 4th.

Intermittent fasting has changed my life. It gives me complete control over my health and weight and emotions around food. It is the Holy Grail for me and I cannot imagine ever choosing to do something else. It is a gift I give myself each day and this gift just keeps on giving in miraculous ways.

I'm living a full life in a body that is now serving me well. It is my temple and I have promise to take care of it, while helping others to navigate their own journey. I am a teacher, a mentor, and someone who cares so deeply about serving others that it feels like something is missing if I do not have someone to guide and teach. **Come aboard the _Fast Factor Circle_ so we may connect and I will be able to share my experience with you more personally.**

Creating Community for Yourself

I'm an introvert. This means that I am able to go for extended periods of time without interacting with other people, virtually or in person. I don't crave socializing and become energized by spending time alone. That suits me as a writer and online entrepreneur, but I'm more than those titles. But I'm still not a very social person.

This said, I strongly believe we benefit from social interaction. Over the years I've refined my views in this area.

While I was in the work force as a classroom teacher and working pert-time in real estate, I was forced to interact with people seven days a week, many of whom I did not care for.

This led to my becoming judgmental, easily annoyed, and unwilling to compromise. Staying to myself as much as possible was the only way I could keep my level of stress to a minimum and to stay as focused and positive as possible.

Coming online as a writer and entrepreneur in 2006 allowed me to rethink my previous thoughts, beliefs, and actions around all kinds of things. I came to the conclusion that I could thrive as an online entrepreneur AND have friends, colleagues, and others I could connect with… online! The Fast Factor Circle that Dr. Ellen Britt, PA, Ed. D and Denise Wakeman run was an opportunity to expand my circle of connections and enjoy a more rewarding intermittent fasting experience.

Here is what one of our members had to say about her experience in this online community:

Janice Dugas' story…

How Intermittent Fasting Changed my Life

Being overweight made me feel bad and lowered my self-esteem to a point something had to be done to gain back my confidence and happiness. That is why I decided to embark in a challenging adventure: changing my eating habits.

In March 2020, I came across the Intermittent Fasting Challenge with Denise Wakeman and Dr. Ellen Britt, PA, Ed.D. They mentioned that intermittent fasting had absolutely nothing to do with a diet; that the teaching was based on science and facts.

The idea to schedule the period of the day when you are eating that best fit your agenda, no matter what you are eating, sold the concept and I joined. With some skepticism, but willing to give it a try. I opted for a 16:8 fasting schedule.

From the time I wake up till it's time to break my fast, I drink black coffee, unflavored water and unflavored tea, and surprisingly enough I do not feel hungry.

As I was putting into practice the teachings from the challenge, I realized how mindlessly I was eating. Often, I was grabbing something in the pantry or fridge not because I was hungry, but to wash away frustrations, stress, and/or emotions. Being a work-at-home entrepreneur, often did I go find something to 'munch' on, simply to get away from my desk.

I lost 15 pounds during the 10-day challenge, and five more in the following weeks. I'm a happy camper and now see myself as a much healthier person and that feels good.

This life changing experience is so much more than just about intermittent fasting, as it deep dives into other essential topics as well such as longevity and natural anti-aging.

I adopted the IF lifestyle and it is no more about the weight loss; it is about improving my health on a daily basis and by shifting my focus to a vibrant "healthy life span".

I am very grateful to Denise Wakeman and Dr. Ellen Britt, PA, Ed.D. for creating this challenge and members of the supportive community which all contributes to us living a more fulfilling existence.

To your health!

Janice Dugas | Member of the Fast Factor Circle

SECTION 4

BEGINNING YOUR JOURNEY

"God, grant me the serenity to accept the things I cannot change, courage to change the things I can, and wisdom to know the difference".

~ Reinhold Niebuhr

If you have decided to give intermittent fasting a try, congratulations. But Yoda taught us that *trying* something is not a commitment with his *"Do or do not. There is no try"* Statement. Once you have made the commitment is when your journey can begin.

First, before you do anything else related to starting an intermittent fasting practice, make an appointment with your doctor to find out exactly what point you are starting from.

While not everyone has a physician as knowledgeable, caring, and detail oriented as I have with Dr. El Tom, you do have someone who knows you personally and is familiar with your medical history, I presume. Work on building a relationship with this medical professional as I have and your body will thank you.

Starting anything during a pandemic is fraught with exceptions to the rule and a schedule that will not be doable once the real world returns to normal.

I'm used to travelling up to ten days each calendar month, both locally and internationally. Back when I was not being cognizant of matters related to my health and wellness, I was used to throwing caution to the wind. But now that I've reinvented myself and lead a very different, and I'll add a more evolved view and perspective, I'm not willing to do anything that will take me back to where I was in my former life.

The idea of being able to control my overall health with intermittent fasting is exciting to me and others I know who are on this journey. The only issue becomes one of learning how to handle issues that arise that are out of my control. I've learned to be more flexible with myself and the world at large. Whereas I prefer to have a schedule that is written in stone, I'm now open to being more fluid, at least up to a point. And, like in the Serenity Prayer, I know when courage is called for, and when acceptance is the right path for me.

This being said, I will still make every effort to eat what and when is best for me, if at all possible. I'll talk about traveling and living with an intermittent fasting practice in a later chapter of this book.

Let's continue, as I share how I have reinvented my life!

CHAPTER 9

Reinventing Myself

"Do or do not. There is no try."

~ Yoda

I believe that we all must reinvent our lives on a regular basis. I've done this a number of times over the past decades, and am sure there will be more reinventions to come during my lifetime. This is an article I wrote about my own experiences with reinvention...

Reinventing Myself... Version 5

My life continues to surprise and amaze me. I've figured out that this is possible because I'm willing to reinvent myself regularly. My first reinvention occurred during the summer before I entered junior high. My most recent reinvention began sixteen months ago, at the beginning of the pandemic and when I decided to lose at least a hundred pounds with a plan that would work for me. Are you in reinvention mode to improve your life?

I've become quite adept at reinventing myself. Currently, I'm in the fifth iteration of reinvention and love the direction life is taking me. If you'll indulge me here, I'll share the story of how I have changed myself from the inside out over the past five decades and used reinvention as a springboard to a new improved life. I've learned valuable life lessons during each of my reinventions and I'll share those with you as well.

Reinventing myself for the first time came during the summer before I went into the 7th grade. Back then, the concept of reinvention was not in the mainstream. Perhaps it was already a "thing" but not in the circles I was a part of or familiar with in my life experience. I just knew I wanted to be somebody else, anyone else, other than who I was. My main focus was around losing weight and having new school clothes.

That summer I learned what a calorie was, how to count the ones I consumed, and that exercise was also an important part of losing weight. I stayed on a strict diet of no more than five hundred calories a day, rode my bike for at least one hour each day, and watched as the unwanted twenty pounds I intended to lose came off easily. Yes, I was starving. But my interest in looking better was stronger than my desire to eat the foods I had gotten into the habit of consuming.

I was earning money by babysitting and doing odd jobs for neighbors and friends of my mother. The weekend before school was to begin my mother and I went to the mall so I could buy clothes, shoes, and an over-the-shoulder purse that was trendy with the junior high girls. On the way home we stopped at the local pancake house. There were having an "all you can eat" pancake promotion and I lost count of how many I consumed that afternoon.

School began on a Tuesday, the day after Labor Day. I can still picture myself in the dress I wore because it became the one for my school photos a month later. It was a dark brown shift, with yellow flowers and some abstract designs in the print. I felt like a hippy, albeit my version was more wholesome and down to earth than the stereotype that was emerging during the late 1960s.

On the first day, a cute boy smiled at me and asked my name in homeroom. Two girls I knew from elementary school asked me to sit at their table at lunch. My mother had agreed to meet me several blocks away after school, and when I spotted her I was flanked by friends, old and new. She said the smile on my face told her it had been a great day for me.

I'd like to say that every day of junior high was just as wonderful as the first one had been, but it wasn't. My reinvention slowly wore off and then it was just like my previous school experiences had been over the years. I was a good student and my grades showed the work I put in to each class. It was relationships with others that made me struggle. By the end of October, I had regained the twenty pounds and then some. When I wasn't invited to a Halloween party hosted by someone I had known for a while, I blamed it on my weight.

The problem with reinventing myself was that I thought it to be an overnight *fix to problems that were always in the background... until they came to the forefront. Life went on, and it would be sixteen years before I thought about reinventing myself again.*

My first husband passed away after a fourteen-month battle with leukemia. He had been a smoker and the doctors at Memorial Sloan-Kettering Hospital in New York City told me this had been a factor in their efforts to save, or at least to prolong his life. Seemingly overnight in my distorted view of time, I became a 28-year-old widow and stepmother to two teenagers. With some Herculean efforts, we all landed on our feet and continue to be close all these years later.

Version 3 of reinventing myself came in the summer of 1992. Hurricane Andrew bore down upon Miami, taking all of my worldly possessions with it and giving me a new respect for Mother Nature. As if that were not enough, six weeks later I was diagnosed with Stage 3 breast cancer and not expected by any of my doctors to survive. I did survive, and reinventing myself was the only way for me to make sense of and to be willing to explore the new version of myself I would share with the world.

In the spring of 2005, I woke up to a feeling I still can't properly explain and describe. It was as if all of my senses were magnified. The colors were brighter, the sounds more complex, the tastes and smells more intricate. Even the tips of my fingers felt different and I found myself caressing fabrics and my pet's fur, as well as my own skin. I knew in those initial moments that something new and exciting was on the horizon. I prayed to God to show me a new way of life, one that would allow me the time and financial freedom to live life on my own terms.

Within a year I was ready to resign from my classroom teaching position and to pass my long-time real estate clients on to others who could better serve them. I discovered the world of online entrepreneur and set out upon a journey of learning and doing things I could not have imagined previously. Each day brought with it new challenges and discoveries in the areas of technology, content creation, and marketing. My world expanded, and with it came increased credibility and visibility. The profitability piece soon followed. Reinventing myself was fun!

But even with all of the newfound success that entrepreneurship brought, as well as becoming a bestselling author soon after, everywhere I went, there I was. What I mean by this is that my weight, and the health issues associated with weighing over three hundred pounds were always with me. Just below the surface, my life was a mess. Much of it I chalked up to age; didn't everyone slow down and begin to experience health challenges as they got older? No. But I didn't have a frame of reference to anything other than what I was experiencing firsthand.

I had moved to a new city, built a brand new home with a gorgeous view of the mountains and canyons, and started a new life. I joined my local Rotary Club and began volunteering with non-profits and other service organizations based both locally and internationally This reinvention, my fourth one to date, felt like the final frontier for my life: it wasn't - the best was yet to come!

In December of 2019 I once again spent several days setting goals to work on and achieve in the new year. For the third year in a row, I wrote down that I would lose a hundred pounds. I hesitated this time, knowing that without a plan my goal would remain a wish and a dream. But something deep inside of me made me believe this time would be different. I couldn't put my finger on it, but I felt so strongly about being able to achieve my goal, and to do it with grace and ease that it excited me inside and out.

The new year of 2020 arrived and I reviewed all of the goals I had set for myself. They were in the areas of health, wealth, relationships, and more, as they were each year. My fingers lingered on the page when I read what I had written about dropping a hundred pounds. How would I be able to achieve this? I needed a plan, and that became my focus around that particular goal.

January came and went, and each week I was again reminded of my goal around losing weight. Now I had edited the goal to include improving my health, but still nothing presented itself as a solid idea or plan. February landed on my doorstep and I vowed to be more focused and mindful around this goal. Every other area of my life was on track; my income was steadily increasing, my creative streak was flowing, my writing was prolific and transformational, and my relationships were flourishing. But each time I got dressed and looked in the mirror, there I was. I was now what is referred to as "morbidly obese" and each day was becoming more of a struggle for me as I tipped the scale at 302 pounds.

In a tiny crevice, deep in the recesses of my mind was the sound of my doctor's voice, warning me about my raising A1C level. He had already begun ordering medications for me, along with various gadgets and supplies. He used the phrase pre-diabetic with me and explained that I would be diabetic within a few months at the rate I was going. I was in complete denial when it came to this. I even told the pharmacist that although I was paying for everything and taking it home with me, I was not diabetic and didn't intend to use anything that had been prescribed for me.

My long-time friend and colleague, Denise Wakeman sent out an email about a 10-day challenge for the intermittent fasting group she hosted with Dr. Ellen Britt, PA, Ed.D. Denise was to be a speaker at my marketing event in Los Angeles during the first week in March. The Challenge would begin the day after my event ended, so I signed up without giving it much thought. At this point in time, I did not yet think of it as a plan, THE plan that could work for me. Instead, I thought of it as insurance, the way many of my prospects do when purchasing one of my courses or programs. I thought of asking Denise some questions about it while she and I were together at my event. I had recommended it to my community and some of the people who had also come aboard would be at my event.

The time came and went and I hardly said a word to Denise about the challenge or even about intermittent fasting. While we were all at the hotel that week, the pandemic grabbed hold. The hotel began to empty out, the flight crews who usually stayed there because of its close proximity to LAX were being sent home, a two-hundred-person wedding on Saturday night cancelled just hours before, and by the following Friday the United States announced a State of Emergency. The thought of once again reinventing myself crossed my mind, and more than once that week.

During the 10 Day Intermittent Fasting Challenge, I saw the light shining down on me. This was my plan, run by people I knew and trusted, and laid out in such a way as to make losing weight, even a hundred unwanted and dangerous pounds to be doable by anyone who was willing to follow Denise and Dr. Ellen's guidance... even me. Reinventing myself saved my life, as well as allowing me to share my story with people all over the world who are now benefiting from my experiences.

I used to attempt to reinvent myself every time my mother and I moved to another apartment and I was at a new school. This gave me the opportunity to try things on for size before fully committing. There was even a time when I tried out different names and asked the new teacher to call me "Jocelyn" or "Billie" or "Stephanie" instead of Connie.

As a young adult, I reinvented with new jobs and friends. But it didn't work. The thing was, wherever I went, whatever I did, and whoever I was, it was still the old me who showed up.

Reinventing Yourself by Choosing a Fasting and a Feasting Schedule

When you're finally ready to give intermittent fasting a try, or to explore it once again if you have already in the past, the first thing to decide is the schedule you will adhere to for your fasting and feasting windows.

For decades, I had believed myself to be someone with low blood sugar. I honestly believed that if I did not eat within no more than thirty minutes of waking up each morning that I would get dizzy, have a headache, and be nauseous. It turns out that is not the case with me.

Now, perhaps I did have experiences with low blood sugar in years gone past, but just as other aspects of our health shift and change as we age, so could this in my life experience.

Because of this discovery that I did not need to eat so early in the morning, I decided to open my "feasting" window around noon each day. Starting with a 14:10 (eating for no more than ten hours out of every 24) and later shifting to an 18:6 (eating during a six-hour period) has worked out well for me.

Also, I became a black coffee and green or black tea drinker, after not having any interest in either of these beverages earlier in my life. I decided that I wanted to have something hot to sip during the morning hours before I began eating, in addition to the water I was used to drinking.

I also added sparkling water to my regimen. I use about 40 percent sparkling, unflavored water when I prepare the bottles I keep on my desk and in my purse at all times.

Those Pesky Hunger Pangs

When you get hungry, taking a few grains of coarse Himalayan Pink Salt on your tongue will help you to forget all about food. I keep a small glass jar of this in my bathroom and in the kitchen. I used to take some almost every day, but over time I've found that the hunger pangs show up less frequently.

Coffee is also a natural appetite suppressant, so I became a black coffee drinker and have some each morning. It tends to keep me awake, so I cut off my drinking at noon each day so I can get to sleep easily around ten each evening.

I also add a tablespoon of organic apple cider vinegar to my "healthy" drink each day. This also serves as an appetite suppressant, even though I do not drink it until after I've opened my eating window. This drink also contains collagen powder and a liquid mineral supplement.

When I shift my "feasting" window earlier or later to adjust my schedule to something outside of my control, I tend to feel hungry at the time I usually would be eating. But this has become less of an issue over time, mostly because I am not alarmed at feeling hungry. None of us is starving and I have rather learned to enjoy the feeling of an empty stomach as I plan which foods I will be preparing and consuming in the coming hours.

Getting "Fat Adapted" for Weight Loss

I have mentioned that I did not lose any weight during the 10-day challenge I initially engaged in during the middle of March, 2020, or even the following week when I had promised myself to eat in this manner.

The reason is that my body was not yet "fat adapted" and able to burn the fat in my body was due to the fact that I was eating or drinking something from soon after I awoke until an hour or so before I went to bed each night.

One of the most overlooked components of fasting is the importance of getting fat-adapted. Fat-adaptation means getting your body in prime condition to begin using fat (dietary or otherwise) as fuel. This is NOT the same as being in Ketosis.

Fasting works (when it works) for weight loss because it shoves your body into ketosis: a state where fats are your primary fuel source. However, just because you're fasting doesn't mean your body will transition easily. Someone with a poor metabolism will deal with much more stress on their hormones. Someone who has already been doing low-carb or ketogenic diets will have a much easier time of it.

Whether you are a man or a woman, get fat-adapted with your

diet first, and use this as your primary weight-loss tool.

Fat adaptation entails getting better at using fatty acids and ketones for fuel as opposed to carbohydrates and glucose.

During this process, the mitochondria become more efficient at utilizing fat for fuel by improving their transport.

When fat adapted, you upregulate genes associated with lipid metabolism by the skeletal muscle. Basically, you get better at burning fat for fuel and your body uses it more efficiently.

Every person is fat adapted to a certain degree but most people's fat adaptation is very poor because of high eating frequency, processed foods, and high amounts of carbohydrates in the diet. This will keep the body locked in a glucose burning metabolism.

Keto adaptation and fat adaptation describe the same thing but they differ in terms of degree. Keto adaptation occurs when the body has switched over to a fully fat based metabolism and requires longer time whereas fat adaptation can be entrained even without ketosis.

Here's how to become fat adapted and teach your body to burn fat for fuel:

Practice Time-Restricted Eating – When you're in a fasted state, you deplete the body from its glucose stores and this makes you run on your body fat. At first, you may feel tired and brain fogged but eventually, as you build mitochondrial efficiency, you'll start feel amazing – healthier and more youthful. You should time-restrict your eating every day by either doing the 16:8 fasting window or eating just one meal a day, known as OMAD.

This is what Robb Wolf has to say about this process of becoming "fat adapted" through intermittent fasting:

Ketosis gets credit for a lot of health benefits. Sustainable fat loss, better energy, a razor-sharp mind—the list goes on.

But here's the thing. If you're not fat-adapted, you won't experience most of these benefits.

Being fat-adapted, although a bit technically distinct from "keto-adapted", means you can effectively use ketones and fatty acids for energy. This allows you to access stored body fat during a fast, and get maximum mileage from a high-fat diet.

I know, the whole ketosis vs. fat-adapting thing is a little confusing. Can't we just pick one term and stick with it?

Not necessarily. Yes, ketosis and fat-adaptation often operate in parallel. But they aren't the same. I'll illustrate with an example.

Take a guy (let's call him Bill) who eats a Standard American Diet. High sugar, high omega 6, few fruits and veggies—in other words, SAD.

One day, Bill sees an ad for keto pills. (Keto pills are exogenous ketones). The ad promises weight loss, so he buys a bottle. When the bottle arrives, Bill pops a handful of pills, his blood ketones rise, and he's officially in ketosis.

So, is Bill fat-adapted?

Not even close. As a matter of fact, he's likely blocking fat-adaptation by taking exogenous ketones. That's because exogenous ketones are <u>well-documented</u> to lower free fatty acids in the blood.

The truth is, fat-adapting takes time and strategy—not supplementation. Today I'll cover the basics of fat-adaptation, what benefits you can expect, and how to structure your diet and lifestyle to promote fat burning.

Being fat adapted basically means being a fat burner. It means that your body can burn fat for energy easily and switch between burning fat and burning carbohydrates.

Anyone who has tried to lose fat knows that it does not usually disappear without putting up a fight. You have to train your body to burn fat for energy.

In our modern society, most people eat a lot of carbohydrates. Our bodies like to use glucose as a source of energy, which it gets from sugar and carbohydrates. Carbohydrates can be burned easily and provide energy quickly.

But when your available glucose runs out, your blood sugar levels will crash. To then get energy again, instead of switching to burning your stored fat, your body starts searching for more glucose.

If you're not fat adapted and run out of glucose, your body will start to break down muscle to turn it into glucose through a process called gluconeogenesis.

On the other hand, if you are fat adapted, your body can take your stored fat and turn it into ketones to use for energy.

There are many benefits to becoming fat adapted. They include:

Burning fat. When you are fat adapted, your body will burn your fat when it doesn't have access to energy from the food you have eaten recently.

You can switch between using fat and carbohydrates as an energy source, which is extra beneficial if you are an athlete or just pushing yourself athletically. If you have carbohydrates before an event or strenuous exercise and you run out of available glucose for energy, your body can switch to burning fat. This will help you to maintain good energy levels for longer.

It will become much easier for you to go for extended periods without food. This is because your body can easily burn your fat. If you eat a lot of carbs, you will become hungry a lot sooner. Being fat adapted makes it easier to do things like intermittent fasting and extended fasting.

Having fewer cravings. Because you have fewer blood sugar fluctuations when you are fat adapted, you will also have fewer cravings. You might have cravings when you first cut out carbs and sugar and start a ketogenic or carnivore diet while your body adapts. But once you've adapted, the cravings should reduce significantly.

Paper Pounds

If you're familiar with author John Green's book, "Paper Towns" for the young adult audience, you know these are the make-believe names added by cartographers to the maps they create to make sure others are not copying their work.

What I mean here by the phrase "paper pounds" is the illusion we all experience when we eat less food, or eat for fewer hours for a few days and the scale shows that we have lost a few pounds. I believe these to be a figment of our imaginations, in that these pounds will reappear on the following day when we consume even a small amount of food or beverages, or we open our "feasting" window for even an hour longer than usual.

In order for me to accept pounds or kilos dropped from my body weight as being real, I like to observe the number on the scale for three consecutive days. Also, bouncing up and down in weight is not an ideal state of being for your overall weight and health.

How Will You Reinvent?

The future is for us to create. It's mostly a blank slate that allows us to write the script of our life story. Perhaps you're ready for great change in your life, and starting an intermittent fasting practice is just the first step.

I encourage you to think about your life in broad strokes, where the canvas is yours to write and draw and imagine the life you wish to live.

Maybe you'd prefer to live in a different part of the world, or to have work that is unlike what you're doing now, or to have a life experience that currently feels too scary to entertain by even whispering it out loud.

Make it happen. I promise you'll be glad you stepped outside the box you made for yourself long ago and you'll find the wings to glide to a new reality.

CHAPTER 10

Living with Intermittent Fasting

Consistency is when you actively practice your discipline. Integrity is the consistency of your words and actions.

~ Kenneth Chenault

Because I began my intermittent fasting practice at the beginning of the pandemic, in March of 2020, I knew that at some point things in the world would open up and I would once again be on the road with some regularity for my personal life as well as for my business.

How would I navigate the waters of going from having almost complete and total control over every waking moment of my time and my eating, to feeling like I was at the mercy of strangers and situations and schedules far out of my control?

Consistency was the first step in gaining control over my life so I could easily start living with intermittent fasting. Staying true to myself proved to be a powerful tool in my quest for the healthy lifestyle I was creating.

Although my primary business and my writing are almost exclusively accomplished online, the work I do each week with non-profits and charitable organizations is done in person. Aside from wearing a mask and maintaining a safe social distance, I needed to figure out how to make my IF practice a natural and seamless part of each day.

I have been able to do this successfully with what I think of as my three-step process. This involves planning my eating throughout each day, remaining mindful, and developing a positive and flexible attitude. I'll go into more detail here so that you can decide what approach might work best for you.

- ◉ Planning: Before I go to sleep each night, I already have a pretty good idea around what I will eat during the following day. I already know if I'll be working at home the next day, whether I have appointments and commitments away from home, or if I'll be engaged in some combination of the two. The Plan is all-important and because a type of blueprint for my day.

If I'll be at home, I choose the foods I want to eat to break my fast. I typically open my "feasting" window around noon or one in the afternoon and have learned to choose fatty foods to eat first thing. This might be a small avocado, a handful of nuts, cheese, or something else like marinated artichoke hearts that come in a glass jar at the market.

On days when I leave home early and drive to another location, I may pack a lunch to have later on in the day. I like almond butter sandwiches, bananas, grapes, cheese, and some crackers like the *Lesley Stowe Raincoast Crisps* from Whole Foods.

If I'll be having lunch at someone's home, a restaurant, or at one of the private clubs I belong to in Santa Barbara, I do not bother to plan what I will order. Because no foods or food groups are off limits, I simply choose from what's available and enjoy my meal. I know that sugary foods are a weakness for me, so I may ask for a piece of fruit or cheese to have while others are eating pie, cake, or ice cream. I've lost my taste for most sweet desserts since beginning the intermittent fasting lifestyle, and for that I am extremely grateful.

- ◉ Mindfulness: Over the years, I've written about mindfulness in my articles and books, and spoken on this topic in relation to mindset many times. Yes, what I'm going to tell you here has a slightly different spin than what will work for authors and entrepreneurs.

Mindfulness requires you to be present in every moment. I've found this to be easier said than done for most of us, so this area of your life must be practiced every day until it becomes a more natural part of who you are.

Early on in my intermittent fasting practice, I shared a story with Dr. Ellen and Denise during one of our Fast Factor Circle calls. I related to them that I had gone into the refrigerator to get some cheese for my dogs when I found myself munching on a baby carrot. This would normally not have been an issue, but at some point in time while I was crunching on yet another baby carrot, I realized I had not intended to break my fast for two more hours!

Others in the group, along with Denise and Dr. Ellen admitted they had done the same thing along the way. I listened intently and observed the behavior involved with this. The reason our leaders no longer had this issue was that they had become mindful of their thoughts, words, and actions and the rest of us had not. I was determined to make changes on a cellular level in this area.

If you've ever left the house, got into your car, driven to the store, come back home, and prepared a meal, and then while you're eating realize you don't even remember leaving the house earlier that day, that's an example of not being mindful. My mindfulness practice began with cultivating the habit of thinking about each thing I was doing, in a way that left an imprint on me. I use as many of my senses as possible throughout each day, and this helps quite a bit.

For example, today I drove to the pharmacy to pick up a prescription for a family member, to the post office to pick up the mail from my P.O. box and to mail two letters, and drove by some friends' house on the way back home to water their plants and bring their mail inside. I listened to the wind when I rolled down the window on the driver's side; I heard a firetruck approaching, pausing, and then driving through the intersection right before I turned into the pharmacy; and smelled somebody's cooking when I pulled into my friend's driveway. I heard the wind chimes when I went outside on their porch to water the plants; felt the leaves of their Ficus tree when I moved the pot over a couple of inches; and saw a black knit cat being worn by someone walking by on the sidewalk behind their house.

⊙ Flexible attitude: I believe we all get to a point in our lives where we want everything done in a certain way. But a rigid approach is typically not sustainable and makes life far less joyous, I have discovered.

Being spontaneous may sound exciting, but you'll have to try it on for size to see how fell it fits your personality. Perhaps meeting yourself somewhere in the middle between spontaneity and rigidness will be best. In any case, begin to think of yourself as being at least a bit more flexible than you've been in the past.

An attitude of being flexible with your eating will carry over to other aspects of your life. This works especially well with young children and elderly adults. Perhaps it's the smartest approach when dealing with all other human beings!

If apricots aren't in season, I'm happy with another kind of fruit. If my banana is too green, I'll wait to eat it another day; if it's already too ripe, I'll eat in anyway or mush it up with some avocado, chia seeds, and a teaspoon of honey and think of it as a pudding treat. No matter what occurs in my life each day, I don't allow myself to be derailed to the point where I would make poor food choices, eat too much (or too little), or eat for more hours than I intended to that day.

Intermittent Fasting with Hotels, Camping, Airports, and Cruises

When I'm traveling, I'm used to planning every detail and not usually having to make changes in my schedule, itinerary, or other plans. Because I've been traveling the world for over two decades now, I was lulled into a false sense of security.

For the foreseeable future, all travel will be subject to change, sometimes with little or no notice. This is where planning, mindfulness, and a flexible attitude will serve you well, in my opinion.

The first hotel I stayed at after resuming my travel in the spring of 2021 was the Hampton Inn near San Francisco, California. I had made my reservation online a couple of weeks before, called them just days before arriving, and then pulled into the parking lot on the day I was to stay there feeling happy and confident.

This hotel chain is known for their breakfast buffet for all guests, as well as a "sack" lunch you may take with you. On this day, the buffet was not open and I had to tell the lady at the desk what I'd like. She assigned me to an open, socially distanced table, brought me yogurt and juice and a toasted bagel with cream cheese and informed me that I could have as much of anything I wanted, from what they had on hand.

My room was on the 6th floor and clean and quiet. When I was leaving the following morning the man at the front desk offered me a sack lunch. I smiled under my mask and thanked him. When I got into my car, I opened the bag to find some delicious and a few healthy treats and I was on my way.

I've now flown across the country more than once, stayed in several hotels, gone camping for several nights, and been on a short cruise. I always have something I want to eat in my purse or lunch bag, so it's almost like I'm testing myself and the world to see if they can throw me a curve that would take me off course for intermittent fasting. I'm not saying that can't happen at some time in the future, but for now I see the future as being clear of any obstacles I or anyone else wouldn't be equipped to handle.

I've also stayed at the home of a few close friends and relatives, and had people stay with me. Though we are far from being back to normal, or at least some semblance of what we all came to know and expect in the past, the skies, seas, and roads are clear for takeoff without any interruptions for our intermittent fasting practices.

CHAPTER 11

Discipline... Getting Back on Track

"Values are related to our emotions, just as we practice physical hygiene to preserve our physical health, we need to observe emotional hygiene to preserve a healthy mind and attitudes."

~ Dalai Lama

It was inevitable that the day would come where I would at least experiment with going back to my old habits around eating.

In Chapter 8 I shared with you my "Walk on the Wild Side." Now let's discuss this further and how it will affect you in the long-term when it comes to your intermittent fasting practice.

As a younger person I took my life and my health for granted much of the time. Perhaps almost everyone does, as it is impossible to imagine being sick or unwell when all you have experienced to date is the state of being healthy and well. Young people are notorious for feeling invincible.

Travel back in time to a period in your life where you had an illness or an injury. Perhaps it was a serious bout with the flu when you were a child. Maybe it was a badly sprained ankle or broken arm. I've experienced all of these, yet my memory is not as clear as to what occurred as I would like it to be. If this describes you as well, use your current intellect to fill in any gaps.

I can remember having the flu during the week of Christmas when I was eleven years old. I had to stay at home, in bed and close to the bathroom for almost a full week. My mother felt so bad for me, but the flu had to run its course and not even Santa Claus could alter the timetable.

But now I'm talking about health and wellness that is under your control. You have the knowledge and the life experiences and the resources to take the very best care of your body, yet all of us fall off the apple cart at some point in time.

Sugary foods have been the ones that I've allowed to derail me over the years. It began when I was a small child, not yet in school and feeling helpless in my surroundings. We were poor, my mother and I and there were times when we did not have enough food to eat, clothes to wear, or even a place to live.

These times of need were infrequent, yet each one brought me back to the previous time. In my mind, I was always waiting for the other shoe to drop and for us to be on the street once again.

My mother's efforts to find a job and a place to live would finally come to fruition, but the trauma to my psyche had already been done. I would withdraw into an imaginary world, where we lived in a beautiful home and had more than enough of everything we needed. It was a dream I kept alive long after these hard times had passed. But it was embedded deep in the recesses of my mind and the memories were always at the ready if I needed them. The final piece of the picture would come when she had achieved some success, and that's when she handed me the prize to make it final.

It was always a Hershey's chocolate bar that she would gently place in my hands. A warm hug and loving embrace followed, and then I was on my own to unwrap and eat the candy. As I'm writing this, I can smell the chocolate, hear the sound of the wrapper being torn off piece by piece, taste the first bite, and feel the tiny squares resting on my tongue. The sensory images remain powerful ones to this day.

Over the decades I have envied people who told me they could live without sugar. I've always asked them if they craved salty foods instead. Some did, but for the most part people either eat to live or live to eat. My intermittent fasting practice has given me a healthier perspective when it comes to food, but every once in awhile I find myself going off the deep end and reverting to behavior that doesn't serve me.

I have now learned to address this head on and to approach my desire to overeat foods that are high in sugar and low in nutritional value for what it is – an addiction that rears its ugly head from time to time, but one that I can get control of within a couple of days.

One thing that I find to be extremely helpful is for me to say out loud that I know I can choose any foods I want, and that I have enough money to buy anything on the store shelves. By doing this, I'm addressing the years of poverty I experienced as a child and I can feel like I have successfully moved past that period of my life.

Get to the point where you recognize what's going on inside of you when you veer off the path. Work on developing a plan and a routine that will take to back to the main course as quickly as possible. We're all human, after all and bumps in the road do not have to derail us for longer than necessary.

SECTION 5

WHAT'S NEXT FOR YOU?

*"To everything there is a season, and a time to every purpose
under the heaven:
A time to be born, a time to die; a time to plant, a time to reap
that which is planted."*

~ Pete Seeger, from the song "Turn! Turn! Turn!",
inspired by Ecclesiastes 3:1-8

Life is in fluid motion at all times. Homeostasis is defined as a property of cells, tissues, and organisms that allows the maintenance and regulation of the stability and constancy needed to function properly. Homeostasis is a healthy state that is maintained by the constant adjustment of biochemical and physiological pathways.

While homeostasis is the goal in the body's quest for near perfection, it is seldom sustained for lasting periods of time.

Entropy – life in chaos and in flux – is the normal state of the world. It is within this chaos that you will find your center. Instead of working towards perfection, think of yourself as an expert problem solver who is super human and in tune with the universe.

Beginning and maintaining an intermittent fasting practice has changed my life and allowed me to reinvent myself from the inside out. Because I started at the very beginning of the pandemic, I have been able to save my life in real time by improving my overall health and wellbeing one day at a time.

Early on, my goal became to works towards being the healthiest and most positive thinking human I am capable of being, based on my age and health history. No longer do I see myself as the victim of illness and injury; these days I know that it is up to me to care for each cell of my body in a way that will make me stronger and more resilient each day. I imagine myself aging in reverse, like the character Benjamin Button. Every sunrise brings the hope and promise of a more youthful body and mind, where anything is possible and knowledge, followed by inspired action is the program of the day.

I wish for you to approach this practice of eating within a window of time each day with an open mind, a loving heart, and a thirsty soul. Welcome the collision of homeostasis and entropy in your life. You can live the life you want and deserve, knowing that your mind and body have the power to carry you through any situation or experience you may encounter.

CHAPTER 12

⎯⎯⎯⎯⎯⎯

Exercise, Meditation, and Self-Care

"Early to bed and early to rise makes a man healthy, wealthy, and wise."

~ Benjamin Franklin

You do not need to exercise in order to lose weight with intermittent fasting. This has been proven for decades, yet I will recommend that you begin at least a regimen of stretching and walking in order to improve your overall health and regain control over your body in a way that will be beneficial to your goals over your lifetime.

As we lose weight, our bodies change. I wasn't comfortable in my skin for most of my life, yet that didn't change when I first began my IF practice because I was not moving my body. Once I did, with simple stretching and adding walking (first for ten minutes and finally, 30 to 60 minutes each day) to my self-care schedule, that's when I fell in love with the body shape and consistency I was creating.

I mentioned Kathy Hicks earlier, as one of the five people who've made a difference in my journey to improved health with intermittent fasting. I'm a part of her daily exercise and body movement program and have benefitted greatly with her tutelage.

She takes us through a series of gentle movement that includes stretching, Pilates, cardio, and weights. All in all, it's a total body workout we can do from the comfort and privacy of our home that has a far-reaching effect on how we think and feel. I have a different body now than I would have had without exercising, even when the identical weight loss I've experienced.

Meditation will help you to focus and to view your life experience as if you're on the outside looking in. Author and Buddhist Practitioner Jack Kornfield tells us to "begin again" when we need a do-over or to change something in our lives. This saying continues to make a difference in my intermittent fasting practice. I meditate each morning for fifteen to thirty minutes during what I refer to as my "quiet time" each day.

My mind naturally wanders during this time, and I open my eyes, thank myself for persevering, and then begin again. If I omit this activity for any reason, I find myself longing for it later in the day. I will encourage you to make time for yourself throughout each day. It's interesting how we find more time in our days and are able to better serve the people and creatures around us, once we commit to caring for ourselves in a loving and nurturing way. Lest you think you are being selfish with these activities, remember that "*He who serves himself, better serves the world.*"

Even when I am buying, preparing, and eating my meals each day, I take extra care to make sure everything is exactly as I've planned. I choose fruit and vegetables containing as few imperfections as possible; my bread and pasta must be fresh and of superior quality; I search for recipes that include ingredients I may not be familiar with; and I shop at stores where I know they have the best interest of the consumer in mind.

Early on I visited a fast-food establishment on a day when I hadn't planned ahead and I was shocked at my experience. Nothing tasted as I'd remembered it and something left a bad taste in my mouth. I realized that I was now finally willing to treat my body like a temple instead of a garbage can. I was worth it, and so are you.

Another way I practice self-care is with a very warm bath. I add a cup of Epsom salts and get in the tub while the water is still running. For the next twenty minutes I feel like royalty and the problems of the world drift further and further away.

Summary/Conclusion

⸻✳⸻

As you've discovered within these pages, developing an intermittent fasting practice holds the potential to change your life. You'll find that you've reinvented yourself over time, even if that was not an original goal.

No matter where you are right now, and what your health and wellness goals are for the near and extended future, I know you will benefit from putting at least some of what I'm sharing with you here into practice.

I recommend you keep reading to go through the Resources section I've carefully provided for you. Check out the people, group, and publication I've listed, knowing that I stand behind anyone and anything I recommend to you.

Then, go back through the book to reread, take notes, and ponder your future with intermittent fasting. Talk to your physician and other medical professionals about this style of eating and living, as well as to the people closest to you in your family.

For me, the intermittent lifestyle is one I intend to stay with forever. This way of eating has made it a simple process for me to drop over 40% of my original body weight, to reverse the Type 2 diagnosis of prediabetes I was given in December of 2019, and to reinvent myself as someone who follows through and is on a quest to live with optimal health and to help others to do the same.

Please connect with me online, and reach out to those I've included here as a part of my village of resources.

May your future be everything you've dreamed of, and so much more!

APPENDIX

Your Quick Start Guide to Intermittent Fasting

"Let thy food be thy medicine and thy medicine be thy food."

~ Hippocrates

I wanted to provide you with a guide to follow along with as you begin your intermittent fasting practice.

- ⦿ Make an appointment with your doctor or other medical professional. Have a discussion with them about the journey you intend to embark on with intermittent fasting.

Make sure they give you a thorough physical examination and go over any details that are specific to your situation and general, overall health. I can't emphasize the importance of this enough.

In my case, Dr. El Tom gave me a complete physical and set up a schedule for tests and blood work at regular intervals: approximately every 90 days. He believed in me and in the importance of my dropping weight from the very beginning, and one of my goals became to not ever let him down. He is a mild-mannered man and it brings me great joy to see him excited at my progress.

- ⦿ Choose the windows of time that you will "feast" and "fast" each day. My recommendation is to begin with a 14:10, meaning that you will fast for 14 hours each day and feast during the remaining 10 hours.

Keep in mind that you are sleeping for seven or eight of these "fasting" hours each day, so it isn't nearly as rigid as it seems.

After a couple of weeks have passed, or when you feel you are ready, consider opening your fasting window to 18 hours, meaning that you will only consume food during a 6-hour window each day. This will make a huge difference in your progress, especially if you are diabetic or pre-diabetic and wish to reverse those effects as quickly as possible.

- ⦿ Discuss your plan with the person or people in your household with whom you typically share food with in some manner. You may be shopping for, eating with, and preparing food for people other than yourself and it will be simpler to begin the conversation with them at the very beginning of your intermittent fasting practice.

In my case, at the beginning of the pandemic, in the middle of March, 2020 I invited family members to live with me until everything improved. This would allow us to form a "bubble" so that we could safely interact with each other. None of us ever dreamed we would still be living together for so long. We have become accustomed to being together and we got into a rhythm that works for us.

I eat one meal each day with one or more of my family members, either a late lunch or an early dinner. They have been supportive of my IF practice and encouraging all along the journey.

- ⦿ Be easy with yourself. Have the patience to allow your body to guide you. I honestly believe that the human body strives for excellence in the background, even while we are doing things to sabotage its efforts.

⦿ Decide what foods you will eat the following day. I have found that if I choose at least some of the foods I will eat the next day, I'm able to stay more focused on my fasting window during the current day.

Dr. Ellen and Denise recommend breaking your fast with something oily and high in fat, so I typically begin by eating some nuts, an avocado, or even some marinated artichoke hearts. Then I move on to my main meal, filled with carbohydrates, protein, and fats.

I have not completely eliminated sugar or carbohydrates from my diet. I do find that I have less of a taste for cookies, candy, breads, and pasta these days, and my cravings for these foods have all but disappeared.

In the beginning, I allowed myself to eat anything I wanted one day a week, but within a month or so this day off lost its appeal. Now I prefer to eat well every day and also to try foods I had not been interested in previously. These include fermented foods and foods that are traditional in cultures outside my own.

EPILOGUE

$\diamond\!\!\!\times\!\!\!\diamond$

As of this writing and as this book goes to publication, I have dropped more than forty percent of the body weight I started at in March of 2020. My initial goal had been to lose fifty percent of my weight, or about a hundred-fifty pounds, but Dr. El Tom had advised me to rethink that goal. I trust him implicitly and will follow his advice.

I believe I may have at least a slightly distorted body image at this point in time, and certainly do not want to do anything to jeopardize my future in any way. The fact that all but four of the clothing items in my overstuffed walk-in closet now fit me is a feeling I did not believe I would live long enough to experience.

I would encourage you to keep a positive and open state of mind as you read through this book. There is no one right way of eating that works for everyone, even though intermittent fasting does check almost all of the boxes for people who are significantly overweight. If this lifestyle could work and be effective for me, perhaps you will have success with it as well.

RESOURCES

Providing my best resources for you is a gift that will keep on giving, if you choose to move forward with your study and practice of intermittent fasting. This list includes the people who I turn to with my questions and personal progress concerns, as trusted resources I can depend on as my intermittent fasting journey continues.

Denise Wakeman and Dr. Ellen Britt, PA, Ed.D. are the leaders of the Fast Factor Circle online group I have referred to many times throughout this book. Without this group and Denise and Dr. Ellen's leadership, I have no doubt that my intermittent practice would have come and gone quickly, as I wouldn't have had the guidance I needed to take what they were presenting to the next level as I did.

Instead, I have become an eager student and continue to learn more about being proactive with my health, physically and mentally. Each month we have a new theme, and the combination of education and fellowship is making a difference for all of us.

Robb Wolfe is a former research biochemist who has functioned as a review editor for the Journal of Nutrition and Metabolism (Biomed Central) and as a consultant for the Naval Special Warfare Resiliency program. He serves on the board of Directors/Advisors for: Specialty Health Inc, The Chickasaw Nation's "Unconquered Life" initiative and a number of innovative startups with a focus on health and sustainability.

Cheryl Major, CNWC is a certified nutrition and wellness consultant and is devoting her life to helping others change their lives by changing what they eat. She was the person who got me started down the path of eating more healthy foods and being mindful of what I put in my body. You may wish to pick up her bestselling book, *Eat Your Blues Away: "Disappearing" Depression by Changing What You Eat* and connect with her to learn more about the ongoing programs and online courses she is offering.

Kathy Hicks is a fitness, health, and wellness coach who pivoted from a career in Civil Engineering to build an online fitness and health business. After working 15 years as an engineer, she decided to not only change her physical fitness level but focus on helping others do the same. Kathy is also an expert in the area of "feet fitness" and has made a difference for my personal journey to health.

David Jockers DNM, DC, MS is a doctor of natural medicine, functional nutritionist and corrective care chiropractor.

Dr. Jason Fung is a Canadian nephrologist. He's a world-leading expert on intermittent fasting and low carb, especially for treating people with type 2 diabetes.

Dr. Valter Longo is the Edna M. Jones Professor of Gerontology and Biological Sciences and Director of the Longevity Institute at the University of Southern California –Leonard Davis School of Gerontology, Los Angeles, one of the leading centers for research on aging and age-related disease. Dr. Longo is also the Director of the Longevity and Cancer Program at the IFOM Institute of Molecular Oncology in Milan, Italy.

Dr. Peter Attia, M.D. is a Canadian-American physician known for his medical practice that focuses on the science of longevity. He trained for five years at the Johns Hopkins Hospital in general surgery, and also spent two years at NIH as a surgical oncology fellow at the

National Cancer Institute where his research focused on immune-based therapies for melanoma.

Mark P. Mattson PhD is a Professor of Neuroscience at Johns Hopkins University. He is the former Chief of the Laboratory of Neurosciences at the National Institute on Aging Intramural Research Program of the National Institute on Aging who has done extensive research on intermittent fasting.

The New England Journal of Medicine (NEJM) is a weekly general medical journal published by the Massachusetts Medical Society that publishes new medical research and review articles, and much more.

ABOUT THE AUTHOR

⟨❈⟩

"Do for a year what others won't; live forever the way others can't."

~ Connie Ragen Green

Connie Ragen Green is a bestselling author, international speaker, and online marketing strategist who is dedicating her life to serving others as they build and grow successful and lucrative online businesses. Her background includes working as a classroom teacher for twenty years, while simultaneously working in real estate. In 2006 she left it all behind to come online, and the rest is history.

She makes her home in two cities in southern California; Santa Clarita in the desert and Santa Barbara at the beach. In addition to her writing and work online, Connie consults and strategizes with several major corporations and some non-profits, as well as volunteering with groups such as the international service organization Rotary, the Boys & Girls Clubs, the Benevolent Protective Order of Elks, the women's business organization Zonta, and several other charitable groups.

As the most recent recipient of the Merrill Hoffman Award, presented to Connie by the Santa Barbara Rotary Club, being honored with this award has strengthened her resolve to serve others around the world in any way she is able to by using her gifts, talents, and experiences in a positive and sincere manner.

Connie credits intermittent fasting with giving her a new lease on life with optimal health and increased confidence.

Connie is the author of more than twenty-five books, primarily around the topics of entrepreneurship, marketing, mindset, and time management. See all of her titles at Connie Ragen Green Books, or search for her books online or in person from your favorite bookseller.

www.ingramcontent.com/pod-product-compliance
Lightning Source LLC
Chambersburg PA
CBHW071132280326
41935CB00010B/1200